Straight-talking business advice:
Brad Burton shows you how to be successful,
by using guerrilla marketing, networking and
a GOYA attitude.

BRAD BURTON

WWW.4PUBLISHING.BIZ

First published in 2009 by 4Publishing
2 The Crescent, Taunton, Somerset TA1 4EA, United Kingdom

hello@4publishing.biz
www.4publishing.biz

4Publishing is a trading style of 4Networking Ltd

ISBN 978-1-907451-00-3

Dedicated to my wifey Kerry
and my three boys Donavon, Ben, Brandon.

A parent's aspirations are lived through their children,
so thanks to my wonderful Mum Brenda, who sacrificed
so much so that I didn't have to.

Roy Hurley – who believed in me when no one else did.

Contents

Foreword

I met Brad through conventional networking and on the face of it we don't make obvious partners: me privately educated from the safety of North Oxford with letters after my name; Brad from the backstreets of Salford schooled at the university of life. Both of us had been successful in corporate life, but when starting out from scratch we both found our ability to do the job was not enough in itself to make a successful business. By combining our different talents and by daring to drop the old-school defensive guard, we have created something dynamic, open and useful for smaller businesses, something we wish we'd had when we were starting out.

So hold on ladies and gentlemen and strap yourselves in for one hell of a ride. This is no conventional business book: this is a hard-hitting, rough and ready guide to the realities of starting your own business. The conventional business book is logical, structured and ordered. It maps out with profound certainty how if you follow its model, success will follow. How come there are so many of these publications? And how come universal success has not been with us for generations? One of the reasons is that life and business are just not that simple.

The territory of business is never so conveniently structured and logical. It is rare to have full and accurate information and, just when you think you have things under control, the unexpected happens. This book deals with these issues in a real-time fashion; it uncovers the real lows and highs of starting out; and it shows you how the unusual and unconventional can be far more effective than the accepted ways of doing things. It jumps about, with stories and insights coming out of the blue, just like in real life.

The central message of the book is this: to achieve things,

stop looking for perfection and take action. This book was written in ten weeks. Would it be a better book if Brad had spent ten months on it? Possibly. But the way the book was written embodies that central message: just get it out there; capture that initial energy, enthusiasm and momentum before it's lost. The long-term benefit of this book? Who knows; and you will never know in your business until you try things – so, to borrow the man's phrase…Get Off Your Arse!

Tim Johnson – Director of Strategy, 4Networking Ltd
MBA, B.Sc. (Eng) Hons
Accredited mediator (civil)
(Cufflinks! – more about that later...)

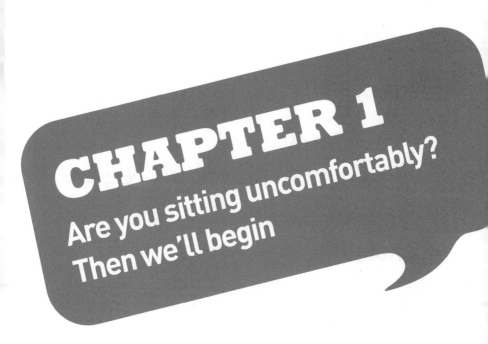

CHAPTER 1
Are you sitting uncomfortably? Then we'll begin

This book is the kind of self help/business book aimed, quite frankly, at anyone...

It is a must if you own your own business, are thinking about owning a business or are in the business start-up phase.

You'll soon see it's written in a different style from most. I'm the kind of guy who is honest, brutally so, sometimes to my own detriment. But I hope you'll find that I'm true to my values and as a result, honest to you, the reader.

You'll find stuff in this book which makes so much sense that you'll find yourself nodding in agreement. Amongst the many things we'll be looking at differently are sales, people, networking, motivation, goals and money.

I'm just a working class lad with (I'm often told) a unique approach to life and business. Throughout my life I've made some bad decisions and, more recently, some pretty good ones.

This book will help you take yourself from inaction to action: sitting on your arse feeling sorry for yourself is not an option. Understand? Right – that's you told, so let's get on with the fun, and it will be fun. However, before we begin, I'll give you a quick CV of my life.

You might already have learned a little about me, but here it is: my life in a nutshell...

Born Manchester, adversity, flashes of brilliance, adversity, heroic failure, dole, dotcom e-brand leader, marketing genius, more heroic failure, adversity, pizza delivery man, MD of largest joined-up business breakfast network in the UK! The lot, inside 36 years.

If you want important sounding three letter acronyms, cufflinks and lengthy reports, I'm the wrong fella. If you're after straight talking, no bullshit, effective business advice from a marketing genius who has been there and done it and is committed to making a difference, you should stick around.

Like you, I've had a fair dollop of adversity in my life, serious adversity. I wasn't sure if I would share it, but I've decided to do so later in the book, to allow you to get a perspective on just how great life can be one moment and how shit things can turn in the blink of an eye when you win 2nd prize in a metaphorical *Monopoly* beauty contest. See, you can't live in fear, we all have one life and the idea is to live it.

If you are in employment, this book will give you some answers to some burning questions. You know the ones. Should I leave? Should I get another job? Should I start my own business?

These are questions only you can answer, but through reading this book, some answers may come to the surface. About business – if you're not making money it's called a hobby.

Private number plates & fish tanks don't make for a successful business. Oh no. Finding yourself *dicking about**, wasting time shopping at the IKEA business centre, deciding whether to buy a red or a blue 99p glass sphere called a *Markta*, instead of undertaking the tasks you need to do in order to succeed.

Back in the bad ol' days towards the end of my PAYE employment in 2004, I lived and worked roughly 150 miles away from my family home. Each evening, before going home to my London digs to do nothing of interest, I used to stick around the office with another disillusioned staffer, having our dinner. We called it 'bleat & two veg'. Have you ever found yourself in a staff canteen or outside with the smokers, whinging about life or a job and how things are not happening? Naturally it's always "somebody else's fault." That's 'bleat & two veg' for you.

Once, indulging myself with another helping of 'bleat', I was gassing with my comrade-in-arms about the fact that whether we worked 80 or 100 hours a week for the company made not one jot of difference to outcomes that held any interest for us. The unattainable house I wanted for my family would still be unattainable, along with the brand new BMW in the drive and the electric gates. Then the penny dropped. Things had to change.

So what was going to change? The company which employed me? Were the directors suddenly going to recognise what an awesome powerhouse of unique talent I represented? How, if they played to my strengths, what an amazing difference I would make to the business and its bottom line? No. That

---

*   **Dicking about:** the things you do when you're avoiding doing the productive 'something' you really ought to be doing.

would suggest the organisation might be obliged pay me what I was worth. So instead, like the rest of the staff, I pretended to work to fill the time, disillusioned with my lot.

In some businesses, dynamic talent is recognised, but not readily embraced. New ideas? We tried those back in 1986 and they didn't work, so we won't try them again.

Maintaining the status quo as an employee means you'll be safe when the next round of redundancies comes up.

I recall the directors asking me to come up with a marketing plan, which I duly did. I broke it down into all the elements needed and I kept it as lean as I could spend-wise, but with adequate investment to make it effective. A few days later, in a meeting where they considered the plan, every single point was thrown out at board level. Why bother asking for something when you don't want the answer?

So the slide began. Resentment building. As head of marketing, I knew my stuff and I knew it would work. Yet everything was dismissed out of hand as "daft" marketing ideas. True, I'm a marketer who has some pretty wacky ideas; they are wacky ideas which work, but require 100% powering through, not 90%. The frustration grew as the bean-counters whose job it was to say "NO" without question, said "NO" at every turn. When you're a staffer in business, it rarely pays to be innovative, as this means sticking your neck out, taking a risk. What if you get it wrong? As a result, most people in corporate businesses just keep their head down, reinforcing a risk averse culture.

Trouble is, it's innovation that keeps a business ahead and there are plenty of hungry competitors out there prepared to take some risks in order to win.

There would be times when the whole team would go to lunch and ask "Are you coming?" My standard response was "Nah, I'm going to finish off this {insert any old task here}." I'd have loved to have gone to lunch with the rest of them, but I could no longer afford it. Microwave rice was on the menu every day I worked in London. Running a home in Somerset plus paying for my London digs plus commuting costs really put a strain on the finances. I was living a hand-to-mouth existence, raiding the 2p jar and explaining to the shopkeeper that I didn't have any coin bags to go to the bank to change them.

Look, let's put this into perspective. This is not like living in a third world country.

Yes, you may be hungry, but you're not going to starve to death. However, it was certainly less than pleasant.

Ever had this experience? You hear the doorbell ringing and answer it to find no one there. Puzzled and slightly uneasy, you are just about to turn round and close the door, but glance down. To your amazement you see a large sports bag and decide to take a sneaky look inside. Eyes flicking from side to side, you check that no one's watching and unzip the bag. Wow, it's full to the brim with £50 notes and orders!

Has that ever happened to you?

No, I didn't think so.

Me neither. Why?

Because it just doesn't happen. Money doesn't just land in your lap.

Ever since Noel Edmonds popularised cosmic ordering, the belief is that individuals can use their desires to "connect with the cosmos" and make those desires become reality...

I assume their fulfilment team has been flat out since then, trying to fulfil all those cosmic orders; I'm still awaiting delivery of my Daytona Yellow Lamborghini *Murcielago* which has been on cosmic back order since 2004.

So, if I really wanted to achieve the things I wanted in life for myself and my family, I had to take control – I needed to start my own business.

A brief aside. If you are reading this, are currently employed and thinking about starting a business — try to get a soft landing. Do your thinking and planning during your employer's time. From my experience, being skint with three days to go before the bank takes the mortgage payment isn't perhaps the best foundation to work from.

So back to my employee story — I walked. On a point of principle, on Friday, December 17th 2004, I told my employers to shove the job up their arse. I'd had enough. A wonderfully liberating and fulfilling experience, until of course I arrived home.

I turned the key in the door, to be faced with my 'supportive' wife, baby son in her arms. She said, "you're home early, is it to look after Ben while I do the shopping?"

That's one way of looking at it.

Another way is that I just quit my job...

Kerry responded, *"You're an idiot! Why couldn't you just have kept your mouth shut for another five days? You could have had your Christmas holiday pay and then sorted out what you wanted to do in the New Year,"* she shouted 'supportively'.

Why? I'm a bloke, that's why. That's what we do: we make

split-second judgments that create ripples well beyond that split-second deciding moment.

Anyways, in the New Year, I'd be setting up my own business; this was clearly the way forward. After all, how difficult could it be? I'm an award-winning marketer. Oh yes boys and girls, back in 2000 at the height of the dotcom boom, I won an e-brand leader award. Granted, not really that relevant as we went into 2005 and yet for some bizarre reason I felt this badge of honour would pave the way to my success.

Where are you in your life right now? What's really pissing you off and yet you're choosing to do nothing about it?

You've a pebble in your shoe: it won't just magic its way out, you've got to do something to get rid of it.

Strangely, for me, it was when the chips were down and I had too much month at the end of the cash, I'd come alive and perform. So, peak performance only came when I was up against it. Crazy. It's almost like the pressure allowed me to work. For most people that doesn't apply, but in my own case the pressure would either build me up or knock me out. Please don't wait until it gets to that stage. Act now and get off your arse.

Go back to being a child — what did you want to be? I wanted to be a car salesman but fortunately that dream was never realised.

Fast forward 20 years and I just wanted to be happy!

Unhappy with life, unhappy with business, what was going to change? I had no control over anything, apart from choosing my actions. Same goes for you. What can you do today to make a difference to your circumstances?

You'll get loads of "no"s in your life, but they don't matter. "No" is different for everyone. It's the "yes"s that matter. The amount of "this time next year we'll be millionaires" I've said in my life make Derek Trotter look like a pessimist.

So I started my first business in 2005 and then... and then... nothing. My standing for a point of principle which had got me to reach this point was now behind me. Now what? I'm self-employed with no real idea of how to make it happen, no 'Janine on reception' to talk to and no support team.

I know what I'll do!

I'll lie on the sofa paralysed with inaction for three days a month.

'MD' — what a great title! I couldn't work out whether those letters stood for 'Managing Director' or 'Managing Depression', as I lay on the sofa, wet flannel on forehead.

I went to the doctor for anti-depression tablets. You know what? In the last three years I've not been as 'depressed', as I assumed I had been. So what's changed? Have I been prescribed some miracle new wonder drug that has no side effects?

I'll let you into my secret: I've been self-medicating.

Are you ready for this? I got off my arse. It's that simple. No whinging about how the world had it in for me, nope,

I GOT OFF MY ARSE.

Over the course of this book we're going to go on a journey, one which will make a massive and positive difference to the way you think, the way you act and the way you perform. We're going to set some outrageous goals. I've made a career of setting outrageous goals.

I attribute this to being active. To stave off that depression you need to do something, anything.

Which brings me nicely on to the next chapter...

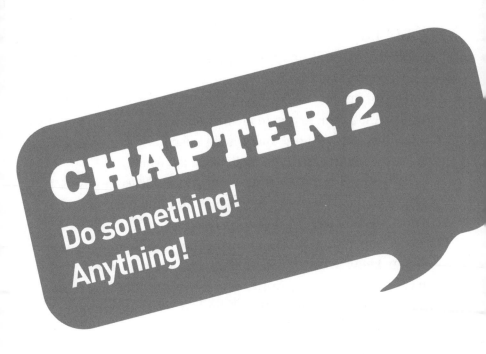

CHAPTER 2
Do something!
Anything!

S o there I am, sitting in my boxroom. A 5x6 foot boxroom, *aggressively waiting* for the phone to ring. Come on phone, ring! Ring! Why wouldn't it ring? After all, I'd placed the *yell. co.uk* advert.

The phone just wasn't ringing. Perhaps there was some kind of fault? After all, the salesperson who sold me the advert said that each month, within my area, there were over 100 searches for 'marketing' and if I got just 10% of them I'd be in business.

And yet, nothing...

So I called up the BT fault line. You know, to check there wasn't a fault on the line. I'd just had my broadband installed, maybe that was the problem. I remembered hearing about something called a 'whoosh test' that engineers do to clear any faults on the line.

Dial 151

"Hello! BT-Fault-line-Sarah-speaking-how-may-I-help?"

"Hi Sarah," and so on

Three minutes later, with my line all whooshed up, Sarah chirpily called back to assure me that there were now no faults on the line. Furthermore, there hadn't been any faults on the line pre-whooshing, so there. Bollocks, now what?

So, going downstairs for a brew and to clear my mind, I began to watch *The Jeremy Kyle Show*. You know the one: the UK equivalent of Jerry Springer. I'm slurping my tea, waiting for those all important DNA results, when my mobile rings.

You know when the boss asks you for that report and you've not done it. Or a sales manager asks for the figures for the month and they are really really bad. Well, it was one of those moments.

My blood ran cold and I was aware of sweat forming.

It's the wife!

Now why would my blood run cold? Let me get you up to speed. I'm an 'award-winning marketer', I walked out of a job, wife says I'm an idiot. I say "I'm an award-winning marketer; I'll start my own biz."

Other small but significant things worth knowing…

1. We have our six month old, Ben, in childcare and Kerry is back in full-time employment at the end of her maternity leave, so

2. She's working full time as the main breadwinner.

3. Childcare costs £6.50 per hour, which we can ill afford. And to top it off,

4. I'm personally £25k in debt, paying minimum payments to the credit card companies, with no sensible and regular income, and

5. I am about to be caught dicking about.

So I pause the Sky+ (yes, we're posh) and answer the phone. "Hi K, I'm on a call, I'll ring you back." First lie of the morning. Having composed myself and created a plausible story, I ring her back. "Yeah, sorry about that, I was on phone to supplier." Second lie. The third, and winning one, was next up. She asks me, "How's it going?"

"OK. Jeremy's looking good: Chantel's from Bradford and she's not sure whether it's Kevin or Derek who is the father of her baby and I'm just waiting for the results, I'll get back to you."

Probably wouldn't have been the smartest thing to say...

So I plumped for a safe bet in the form of a simple "fine". "That'll get me off the hook," I thought.

Let me share a little secret with you. When someone says their business is "fine", they're in big shit, so make sure you have your terms & conditions in place 'cos you ain't getting paid.

"Fine, I got a load of irons in the fire."

At this point Kerry adopted 'supportive wife' mode and pointed out:

"When HSBC take irons in the fire for mortgage payments, I'll let you know. Until then, you're going to have to do something."

In life, do you recognise that feeling when you are avoiding something and keep walking backwards, with the cliff behind you? There comes a point when you have no cliff left. This was one of those moments. That evening Kerry looked for a 'suitable job' for me. I was in luck: supportive wifey had found me one.

In this case Lady Luck appeared in the form of a job delivering pizza for £6 per hour at The Pavilion on the seafront at Burnham-On-Sea, Somerset. As you may imagine, I was ecstatic. Nevertheless, I still had to go through a rigorous telephone interview. It went so:

"Can you ride a moped?"

"Yes."

"You've got the job."

So, from Monday to Friday, this award-winning marketer would be out there punting his consultancy. On Friday, 6pm-11pm, I'd be delivering pizza.

Par for the course, it all went horribly wrong. I rang a doorbell and wallop!

Standing in front of me was the very client who had given me the job of managing their marketing, just two weeks previously.

"Brad, hello, what are you doing here?" (Another blood-chilling moment)

"As I was passing on a Saturday night, I just thought I'd drop off the initial creatives of your logo. By pure fluke I happen to be wearing a daft cap and carrying a pizza bag complete with the piping hot pizza you just ordered. What are the chances of that?"

I actually span some bull about working on a DM (Direct Marketing) campaign for the local pizza company and wanting to get a hands-on approach to the biz to get a feel for how they operated...

He knew I was lying, I knew I was lying, but what could we do?

I even got a £1 tip. This stuff writes itself really.

Not my finest hour. But why the guilt? Trying to keep the wheels on my life? There is no getting away from it, however much you might want to – business is tough. It is tough. If you have savings, they dissipate at the same rate as your self-belief.

"Do something. Anything" is all about changing surroundings in order to thrive.

Every Friday night, dealing with pizzas, or rather not dealing with them, I used this time to think, to plan, to adapt.

Time is only wasted time if you choose to waste it. I turned a situation to my advantage. You can do the same.

Have you ever been into Tesco's and looked in the chilled meat section? Looked at a nice lamb cutlet and thought "Lovely! That'll be nice with a few new potatoes, veg, and a dollop of mint sauce for Sunday lunch." You simply grab the shrink-wrapped cutlet, pop it into your trolley, go to the check out, the lady behind counter moves it over the scanner with an audible beep and swipes your credit card. The aforementioned meat is thus one stage nearer to going under the grill and being plated with those new potatoes.

Mmm, lovely. Employment is a bit like that.

Self-employment on the other hand goes a bit like this (if you're a vegetarian you may want to skip this next paragraph):

You get up at 3am, dress head-to-toe in camouflage fatigues, drive to the nearest rural area, leave your vehicle, mooch over fences and hedges in order to find a sleeping lamb. You snake up on your belly and give it an almighty crack around the skull with an 8lb ball hammer. Next, you pull out its innards with your bare hands and take a bone-saw to its bloody little corpse in order to steal that lovely shoulder cutlet.

OK, probably an extreme example, but the principle is the same. When we're employed we just have to do 'our bit' and we do it really well. All of a sudden the transition from being a staffer to being self-employed is a tough one. You don't have just the grill to tend to; you have to go out and find the stuff to feed it, and yourself.

Then, back in November 2005, a contact I'd met through one of my clients gave me a *'pssst!!!'* moment, a cloak and dagger invite to a 'networking group'.

What the hell *is* a 'networking group'?

Apparently, it's a group of business people who pass each other leads and look out for each other. This sounded just what I needed. The very thing that could break the cycle of my self-employed isolation trap.

Sounds great, I'm in!

"When is it?" I asked.

"6:45 in the morning," said my contact.

"Geezuz, why so early?" He fired back: "Do you want more business or what??" Fair comment...

"I'm there!" I said, gratefully.

I arrived. Thirty people in the room.

Pretty damn good.

Euphoria! This really was what I needed: a world where I had points of contact and a voice. We sat down to breakfast and each of the attendees stood up in turn to speak for 60 seconds. Trepidation reached fever pitch as it was finally the visitors' (I being one of them) turn to speak. My debut duly arrived. I had what I was going to say all scribbled down and knew it'd be fine.

I stood up and began to read.

"Hi I'm Brad Burton, I'm a marketing genius, my company is called 4Consultancy, we're a..."

"SIT DOWN"

I laughed, assuming it must be some kind of joke. I carried on.

"We're a..."

"PLEASE SIT DOWN! One of our members is a management consultant; therefore there is a conflict of interest. PLEASE! Sit down and we will resolve this at the end of the meeting."

I said I was not one for three letter acronyms, but this was a real *"wtf?"* moment.

My initial enthusiasm was slammed down when I was rounded on by a 'Chapter Director' (no less!) and a 'Dispute Co-ordinator'. They explained that the norm in networking was to have a 'category lockout'. This in effect meant that each group could have only one person from each profession within its membership at any one time.

Giving someone a 'Dispute Co-ordinator' badge is like making them the Hall Monitor at school who seeks outs pupils running around when they should be walking; Dispute Co-ordinators like to seek out and find disputes. It's their job. In my opinion, it's barely one step above giving out parking tickets.

It seems there was a chance of being offered a 'seat' if I changed my company name from '4Consultancy Limited' to '4Marketing Limited'. The problem the management consultancy member had with me, apparently, was with the 'c' word, 'consultancy'.

I asked the question, "Am I the world's unluckiest man or is it common practice in business networking to make visitors feel really, really uncomfortable?"

No one said that yes it was, but I got the impression that yes it was, particularly if your profession conflicted with that of an existing member. I suppose if you pay out £500 a year for the chance to blow someone's head off, then there's a real hunter thrill when your opportunity to get good and bloody comes up.

I did try to join, but had my letter, along with my cheque, sent back. They said my application had been denied due to a "conflict of interest". Honestly, I was totally gutted. I wanted to belong; no, I *needed* to belong to something and I was adrift in the sea of self-employment, not sure whether to have my anchor down or my sail up.

Amazing, isn't it, how different things might have been had there not been a member in my profession locking me out. Hang about, there wasn't! I was a marketing consultant; the other bloke was a management consultant...

Pah! Anyways, I thought I'd throw that in for you to read because I'm often asked about the history of how it all began. Well, there you have it, the whole truth and nothing but the truth, so help me God.

As a result of a need to "do something, anything," 4Networking was born. A networking group with a difference. A difference that was going to change my life for the better and all those it touched. But had I not experienced that adversity, 4Networking would never have been born.

Absolutely crazy! Think about that...

Good comes from difficult and unpleasant situations in life.

In fact, I've just thought of something pretty bizarre/profound (delete as applicable), which I'll share with you:

If it wasn't for that nutter Adolf Hitler, you wouldn't be reading this book.

Germany invades Poland, WW2 kicks off and the Yanks come over to the UK. So in 1945 Sergeant Walter Loving of the United States Marine Corps comes over to Blighty. He kindly gives my gran bubblegum, cigarettes, bananas and finally a good ol' *Yankee Doodle Dandy*, before pissing off back to Virginia, U.S. of A.

The Allies win the war. Hitler is defeated. Hurrah! Mr Loving leaves gran with soon-to-be born baby. Baby is my future dad, my dad meets my mum, now fast forward 36 years and you're reading this book!

See, that's just mind-blowing! Every single action sets you on a pathway to your future. I bet you can come up with a seemingly innocuous decision you or someone else has made that has had a profound and positive impact on the lives of you and your loved ones.

Seriously, if they ever invent a time machine to take out Hitler, I'm going to be removed from history. I'm sure *Mein Führer* is on many a *Time Lord* assassins' hit list, along with Cliff Richard.

About your decisions: you never know how groundbreaking they will be until they're in the rear-view mirror. Enjoy this life and enjoy those decisions.

Back to 4Networking: it wasn't going to be snooty; after all I'm a working class lad. I couldn't and wouldn't compete on the old class level. It would be an honest network that made everyone feel comfortable, a network that had as flat a structure as possible whilst still maintaining order.

Networking with *forced referrals* creates 'Aunt Doris' referrals.

Aunt Doris wants new decking for her patio. Well, not really, but lobbing in this referral gets me off the hook for this week's meeting. Of course you are obliged to warn Doris, "If someone rings you up talking about decking, just tell him you are now waiting until next summer." If you insist on sticking people in a straitjacket made of your rules but without their buy-in, they'll find endless ingenious ways to play a game of 'obeying your rules' in a way that suits them.

So instead we worked on creating a network which was self-policing, with invisible guidelines. We wanted to create a culture where members rowed their own boats, as relying on third party referrals for the success of your biz is lunacy.

4N was born out of necessity. My necessity, at the time. As I mentioned earlier, there comes a point in life where you run out of cliff. I had recognised that I needed people and I needed appointments. And if you are in business, so do you.

Here are a few things that worked and really helped to keep me on track and focused during those early days.

Send five letters a day

Something I landed on early doors. This gave me focus, even if it was just getting the data, printing the letters, licking stamps and going to the Post Office. There's something wonderfully fulfilling and rewarding about getting the post off. You are doing something positive and you are moving forward. As an appointment-getter it's pretty ineffective to be honest and it's highly unlikely you are going to be flat out with enquiries. But I did get some and from those would spring further nodes of opportunity.

Five cold calls a day

Geez, I hated this! Well, in fact, some days I relished it. Other days it terrified me, but cold call you must. So here's how you do it. Get a list of potential targets — Google is your mate for this. Grab a database and once you've done that, don't allow yourself the luxury of fiddling to get it perfect, just get it going. OK, listen up. Database building should not be used as a half-baked excuse for dicking about. Spend just 30 minutes on it and get yourself five points of contact. Now, here's the tough bit. It's down to you to call. I'm not going to lie; it is tough, unless you're a nutcase. Telemarketing is one of the few professions where it helps to be mad.

So, big deep breaths, just three of them, and then count down out loud: 10, 9, 8, 7, 6, 5, 4, 3, 2, 1 and then begin dialling the first number on your list of five.

"Hi XX, I'm YY from YY Co. I've been looking at your website and I thought it'd be worthwhile us having a sitdown for **10 minutes** (the 10 minutes is important) sometime next week to tell you more about XXX."

Keep it brief, keep it laser-beam focused and offer them a 10 minute appointment. We'll talk more about the power of the 10 minute appointment in Chapter 12. Problems come up if you over-egg the pudding. You will get blown out loads of times but remember, as you will learn as we go on, "It's the "YES"s that matter, not the "NO"s."

Try this for a week.

Go to lunch

"I can't spend time on lunch; I can't even afford lunch." Look, I'm not suggesting you go to Heston Blumenthal's Fat Duck every day; after all you don't get paid for sick days.

/cymbal crash

I am suggesting that at least once or twice a week you take time out to grab a bite to eat with a client, a friend, or a friend who's a client and use that time to live it. Use that time to bounce off your thoughts and feelings. This is something I did, often four times a week. It's not by accident I have a cholesterol score as high as I have. "Points certainly don't make prizes in the cholesterol game of life." Thanks Brucie.

The routine of going out to lunch changes your surroundings and provides a brief reprieve when "everything is fine". Going out often meant visibility at the restaurant I used to frequent; the staff got to know me, as did the regulars, and I used it as a networking opportunity.

You see, I've been there and done it. Going out for lunch is easy, it works and if there's a better way to cure isolation and improve your morale, let me know.

Force yourself to do something, anything, different.

Give yourself goals that are both unattainable and attainable.

Get your wins where you can; what do I mean by this? When you get your first cheque, a new client, pay off a bill, receive a new enquiry, meet someone new, this builds your hopes up. Really use that hope and positive energy as a kind of relay race to carry you to your next win. Visualise where you want to be and how you are going to get there.

When you're self-employed, every day is a work day, every day is a bank holiday. Work when you are in work mode. Chill when you are not.

Go watch some telly, do something different, anything, and don't feel guilty. OK?

Don't go into a shell and don't let depression and self-doubt soak in. The answer is within you, every single day. So speak to people; bounce daft ideas off friends and family. These guys are the ones that you are going to need to have faith in you and support you whilst you get yourself and your business off the metaphorical bicycle stabilisers. They really do need to believe in you, believe you know what you are doing. And when the shit hits the fan, which it will, they will still believe in you, knowing what you're doing, even if you don't.

Really stuck?

Not sure what to do?

Cold water may be the answer!

This is amazing...I've been sat looking at my keyboard, 'dicking about' online for 20 minutes, uncertain how to progress. Then a mad idea surfaces.

I go to the sink, fill a one litre bottle with cold tap water and then pour the icy water all over my head. This becomes unbearable after a few seconds. However, it's worked. It did exactly what I thought it would do. It's reset my thinking completely: the bottleneck in my head that had been stopping progress the minutes before this self-dunking has now shifted. Whatever the hold-up was, it's now gone.

I've come back to my keyboard and I'm good to go! Radical & free motivational tool! Try it, it may just work and it doesn't cost anything.

You do end up with a wet head, but hey!

That's what towels are made for and remember:

Daft ideas sometimes work.

I remember being laughed at on numerous occasions when I talked about 4N becoming the largest joined-up business breakfast network in UK.

"Don't be silly, business networking is a closed shop." It may well have been.

Not anymore. Daft ideas sometimes work.

CHAPTER 3
Make it happen

S o we've done something, anything, with the intention of finding answers. As a consequence additional questions will come to you.

So now we need to 'Make it happen'. This is the time to give it your best shot, which will achieve one of two things:

Results or reasons

1. Results, what you aimed for is achieved. Woohoo! Good times!
2. Reasons explaining why it didn't happen this time out. Reasons are good, because they move you forward and you now make future calls based on your informed experience and knowledge.

Now you have some answers, it's time to make some moves.

Make your daft ideas happen. We'll only know if they are truly workable or truly daft by undertaking them and making them happen.

So we're going to create some lists. These lists help you with the preparation needed to give it your best shot.

So, lists. I need you to grab pen and paper...

No really, this is very important, don't just hoof this bit, think "I can't be arsed" and bundle on through without it.

Get off your arse. I'll wait.

Right, so you're armed with a pen; I want you to write a list of things on the left hand side of the page, one thing on each line. I want you to write at the top in BIG letters:

TO DO TODAY LIST

You don't need to put things like:

1. Make a cup of tea
2. Watch Jeremy Kyle
3. Fib to 'supportive wife' about the biz being "fine"

Those things happen by default, so we need to jot down a list of the 'things I can do today'. We are not looking at things you would like to do if you had a bigger marketing budget or had more staff; we are just after things that you can undertake today to move your business, and as a result your life, forward.

I'll start you off, a few blasts from the past aka the last chapter:

1. Get Googling, find some prospects in your area
2. Draft a letter to send to prospects
3. Print and send five letters today (Top tip: handwrite the envelopes – gets much better results)
4. Make five cold calls

Right, now it's your turn...c'mon! You can do it.

I've given you four, let's have another ten from you and you're good to go.

So now you have a list of stuff to do today. Get on with it. Make it happen.

Doesn't that feel good? You are no longer adrift at sea. Now I recognise by this time it may be late in the day. As 5pm draws closer you need to know that when you work for yourself, evenings are just another part of the working day. The great thing about being self-employed is that you get to choose which 18 hours you work each day.

From time to time I come across serial planners; they'll still be writing the **To Do <u>Today</u> list** during *Corrie*.

You know the ones? They're forever enrolling on college courses, always using a lack of accreditation as to why they can't progress a business or an idea. Chase, chase and chase the next certificate. I've a friend, in the interests of anonymity we'll call him 'Robin', he's always at it, a serial planner. You'll know people just like him. Always creating business plans, dicking about, preparing and working on Excel documents showing year one, two and three projections and yet he's not even beyond his first month.

Let me share something with you boys and girls:

It's easy making money on spreadsheets: I've done it hundreds of times.

A quick tap of the key here, add a three there and wallop. I'm a *spreadsheet millionaire*.

Robin never does anything with these immaculately presented business plans; they do look and read great though. But they may as well have a foreword by JK Rowling; they are effectively works of fiction.

We never had a formal business plan with 4Networking. Nope! All upstairs, /taps head. The only time a business plan got written was when we were going for the Small Firms Guarantee thing for £70,000. After going through some seriously fiery hoops, the banks then wanted us to personally guarantee the lot which all-in-all seemed a bit of a farce. So we kicked it into the long grass and decided we'd go without the money.

Guess what? We're still here. In those situations, I think it's worth asking yourself, do you really need money from the banks? After all, it's a massively long and drawn out process, which is no good if you need capital fast.

Anyways, back to our friend Robin. What he needs to do is find a Batman (well I thought it was funny), someone he can team up with so that he can do what he's good at: planning, thinking and preparing whilst the caped crusader does his 'KA-POW!!!!!' thing.

Equally, every Batman needs a Robin. A dynamic duo which you can rely on to take on the world.

My friend, he's actually called Tony, would make an excellent 'Robin', but he needs to get involved with a team that needs someone like him. The Tonys of this world ensure steadiness and focus. Success in life and in business is down to teams being an eclectic mix of people. In today's world, certainly using a network like 4Networking, having your own company team in-house is not the big deal it perhaps once was. It's now possible to assemble a virtual company fast, without all the costs and hassles associated with setting up a real business with real employees.

Establish whether you are a Batman or a Robin and be happy.

Gordon Brown was unhappy being a great Robin, yet I think it's fair to say, he's certainly not made a great Batman.

Both roles are equally important. I've lost count of the number of times my 'Robin' (aka 4N's Director of Strategy, Tim Johnson) has saved my Bat-arse when the superhero in me has bitten off more than it could chew or when I overreached myself and my exuberance has left me exposed to risk.

So if you can relate to this, please stop all the accreditation chasing, unless of course your business really needs it.

I don't have a qualification to my name; I've a few D and E GCSEs knocking about and my CV probably has them as 'A's and 'B's. It's so long ago, I can't remember the grades, but who cares? But can I do it? "Do it", in this case, is swanning around the UK eulogising about 4N or writing a decent book. Well, you can be the judge of the latter.

Sometimes you don't need qualifications to do a job. You just need to do the job.

If you can do the job, you're qualified.

Unless of course you're the pilot of a Boeing 737 or a brain surgeon operating on me, in which case seven years in university and a bit of hands-on practice on someone else please.

I'm 36, at the time of writing; I've had two stints on the dole, a combined total of about four years collecting benefits.

I'll be frank, I've lost my way a couple of times in life, as I'm sure we all have.

Even back then I made things happen, spending four mornings a week in the library. I read the broadsheets, books on management and other business stuff (this was before the internet really existed as we know it now). I got myself an education, a self-taught foundation which to this day has formed the roots for all that I do. So, stop looking for excuses as to why you can't do something, stop talking, get doing; tell the world *why you can do it.*

Give yourself a deadline or a time when you will begin. I do this all the time. I give myself daft timescales because otherwise something more important comes up. If it was significant enough earlier to have added to your list, don't allow yourself to get blown off course.

Speaking to a friend of mine, Paul Norman, *www.orangetreedevelopment.co.uk*, about this subject, he said "I am of the same view. Never, ever, do nothing. That is the absolute characteristic of business in the UK, it just drifts. Obviously, if you can see the likely outcome of what you plan to do, so much the better, but I am a big advocate of constant energy, driving forward. Keep up the pace and, although from time to time you will have just discovered an idea that won't work, at least you won't be doing nothing. And the next idea will work or the same one, but tweaked."

Genius, I think you'll agree. Someone who gets it, this principle of 'making things happen'.

Making it happen, I now live this attitude. I recall doing several of the 4Sight slots at 4Networking meetings. 4Sight slots are a member's insight, not a sales pitch, for 10-20 minutes slap bang in the middle of each of these breakfast group meetings. Anyway, in November 2008, I undertook about ten of these speaking gigs in a row up and down the UK. After nine of them, I was approached by a member of the group who said I was "inspirational" and "motivational". Which is absolutely nuts. When we first started this thing, I could barely string a sentence together and was effectively a fat bumbling idiot. What's changed? *Boom, boom!*

So with that, the cogs started turning and one evening whilst having a drink, following the Business North West trade show in Manchester, I asked a mate of mine, Warren Cass of *www.BusinessScene.com* fame, a question:

"How do you become a motivational speaker?"

He said:

"Create a website and say you're a motivational speaker."

So I did just that. *www.bradburton.biz* was born within a week, along with delivery of 2000 plastic business credit cards, featuring a daft image of me winking with a pizza box. No business plan as such, no Excel spreadsheets, no projections.

Wallop, next thing I have bookings coming out of my fat arse. You couldn't make it up.

Those ten groups I 4Sighted at didn't exist back in February 2006. In fact no 4Networking groups did.

Just a daft idea

Starting from the industrial town of Bridgwater in Somerset back in Feb 2006, eight miles from where I lived, I managed, from a standing start, to get 72 people to the launch of what was set to become a UK networking phenomenon. Did I honestly know that back then? No, of course not. But it still didn't stop me opening with the line "Welcome to the future of business networking."

You need to go balls out every single time. It's a strategy that works for me, that is, telling people what I'm going to do and then making it happen, or look pretty stupid. It may work for you, it may not.

You never really know the outcome of anything on which you embark. The only time you know, is when you know.

So, in the two weeks preceding the launch, I looked at the database I had built up from my hobbling-along marketing business. I then hit the phones: speaking to anyone I had previously spoken to, telling them all about this brand new networking group, which would get rid of every element that people disliked about networking, whilst expanding on the stuff they liked.

To each person I contacted, I did what I call my 'Colombo close', a little trick which works beautifully. Just as the other person thinks the conversation is about to end, you say "OK, bye" and then jump in with "Oh, and another thing, (their name), do you know anyone else who might be interested in coming along?" Seven times out of ten they'd give you another name. I'd do the same trick with the contact they'd give me, woohoo, an everlasting prospect list. Do consider how you can incorporate that into your business. It works.

So fast-forwarding to the day before the launch: myself, the 'supportive wife' and mum were all hands on deck in my two-bedroom house in Somerset, printing, cutting and folding placeholders and badges ahead of the launch of 4Networking at 8am the next day.

We finally finished at about 1am. I dropped my mum off and went straight to bed when I got home. I didn't sleep that night; racing over and over in my mind, not about the day, but the bit where I had to speak in front of an audience. The last time I'd done that was at the Institute of Directors in 2000. Back then, at the height of the dotcom boom, I worked at an ISP (Internet Service Provider) as head of marketing. The PR team got me a speaking gig, on stage with the MD of Freeserve. It was an opportunity not to be missed. Well, it would have been if I was any good at speaking in public. I'd done no preparation. The PR firm had written the Powerpoint and I did everything wrong. I mean everything!

However, I was on what I call an inevitable conveyor belt, with the day of reckoning looming.

I don't do 'formal' at the best of times, but this was a new level. Anyway, I stood up at the podium, lights beating down, and I died. Oh my God, I died! A 20 minute presentation that was ill thought-out; even worse, it wasn't even my material, quickly mumbling through and reading each of the slides whilst sweating like a criminal and looking at my clutch foot. I couldn't get off that stage fast enough.

Never ever again.

Until five years later, 73 booked, 72 attend the 4Networking launch, where, I'll be honest, we made all manner of boo-boos, even forgetting to take the £10 from each attendee to cover the venue costs, so that's a pretty good howler. This was followed by 72 people all having 40 seconds each to speak; time ran out at about the same time as the attendees' patience.

After the 40-second round, we had a speaker scheduled and then something we called the 'Let's Talk' round. This was where each networker could complete a small form and then, one by one, walk up to people in the room they wanted to speak to or could help.

Do the math, we just wouldn't have got the 'Let's Talk' slips out within the two hour meeting timeframe and anyway, it was boring the tits off everyone. Then a 3M *Post-It* moment, when 4N's newly appointed Director of Strategy, Boy Wonder Tim Johnson, took control, saying "clearly this isn't working" and to "make your way to the people you want to speak to."

The birth of the 10 minute one-to-one appointment. Darwin's evolutionary theory needed to move on a few generations. But that first Bridgwater amoeba sparked off something pretty spectacular in networking terms.

Come to think of it, we were both newly appointed directors. The company was formed on 17th February 2006, the day after the launch event on 16th February.

It was formed to cash our first membership cheques; back then, single group membership cost £250 per year. Of the 72 attendees at that first meeting, our first two new members stepped forward to join. Out of interest, both these pioneer 4Networkers were members from the very networking group I was bundled out of.

A migration, which was a sign of things to come. It was clear even then that there was a large space in the market for a more approachable, different kind of business social/business network.

Knowing what I know now, if we held that launch again, I reckon 30+ would have joined — you learn.

4N was started with £0, we sold our first two memberships and bought some 'You are invited' cards with

the money.

Call me old fashioned, but isn't that the way a business should be built?

Investment's all very well. In the early days of 4N, we had a speculative enquiry from an investor who wanted to place £300,000 with us. Now that's terrific, but aside from a Range Rover *Sport* with 4Networking logos all over it, on what could we have spent that money? Well OK, we could have spent the money, but on what?

That's what I call making it happen.

We'll come back to Tim and the importance of mixed teams in Chapter 5.

At that launch I had two people laugh in my face; famously one of them said "It'll never work". Those words galvanised me beautifully in the same way as when a history teacher told me as a teenager that I'd "never amount to anything", although up until recently, Mr Rogers, you were probably right.

I'm sure you've had a similar objection or at least a "Don't be silly" whacked in your face at some point in your life, whether as a child or as a young person. You may have heard the "Don't be silly; what do you mean you want to be a police officer? Why not go and work at the car factory? Your dad's worked there for 40 years" mentality.

But it's down to you to make it happen. Use the naysayers that put down your ideas and do some mental aikido with it, to spin that negativity into positivity, and in your favour. Turn the tide.

Drop the requirement to feel great,

accept it's never going to be perfect, just get it started.

So how are you going to make your millions? It is millions you're after, right? After all, that's why you are working 18 hour days.

So what are your goals, aspirations, dreams and motivation?

Let's begin with motivation. When we lived on Tesco's 8p beans and *Value Range* bread, money was a major motivator.

Why? Because I recall hiding my 'mechanically recovered' fish fingers. Nope. I've no idea what that might involve either, but it doesn't sound great. Don't believe me?

Look at the ingredients on the side of a cheap packet of fish fingers, like those which I had hidden under a box of premium *Crunchy Nut Cornflakes*. For that brief moment I had sanctuary; a world where my supermarket shop wasn't a hunt for the cheapest item. Then *wallop*, as my Kellogg's brand shield of success was removed and duly beeped and bagged, revealing to the people behind me in the queue my true status.

Blue and white striped *Value* packaging; mealtimes of bread with everything.

Right, back on track: motivation. I used to think it was money, and back then it was. Money was needed to get myself from feeling like a failure every time we did the weekly shop. Now I sometimes buy Tesco's *Finest*, which is close to *living the dream*.

My motivation has changed, evolved, moved on, with a focus on making a difference. A positive difference, and guess what? As a result, money-making is inevitable: a by-product of doing lots of great things right.

So, honestly, right now, what's the first word that comes

into your head when thinking about your motivation? The likelihood is that that first word is your true motivation. So, we need to use that as the endpoint which means something to you. Everything you intend doing, you will do in order to make your dreams a reality.

I think most people would be happy pulling £200 a day. Really, is that so unattainable?

So let's start with that question: how can you clear £200 a day?

Look, you may want to clear £2,000 a day, heck, even £20,000 a day. But it all starts with a target.

If you do want to clear £20,000 a day, why? Ask yourself again. Why? What is your motivation? Do you really need a *Sunseeker* yacht?

Even to this day, my mum still says, "Don't build your hopes up, Brad, just in case it doesn't happen." It's probably the single piece of advice I refuse to digest from my mum. I make a point of building my hopes up every single time. Why? Because it's like a hope relay race; just as you are running out of puff with one baton of hope, the next one is just in reach to power you on.

My motto is...

Shoot for the Moon, you'll never hit it. So what? You're aiming for it!

Yours, free — an exclusive cut-out-and-keep
Brad Burton bookmark.

CHAPTER 4
Meet – Like – Know – Trust

"4Networking doesn't work."

Well that's what somebody once levelled at me at a breakfast networking meet. He requested a 1-1 appointment slot and I accepted.

Do you ever get the feeling you're going to be mugged? 10 minutes of burnt ears later, he comes up for breath.

Remember the old CB radios from the 80s, where you pressed the button on the side of the microphone to transmit, which in turn meant you couldn't receive? That was what it was like. Now, this was a problem.

Our friend, we'll call him Mr Z, had recently bought a business, a printing franchise – and he'd paid £42k for a 'book'. Don't know about you, but I'd want it signed by the Holy Trinity and Barack Obama for that sort of money. I'll get onto the 'franchise thing' later.

Now, the crazy thing is I knew someone from within the network who had bought into the *same franchise* and had, just a few weeks previously come up to me and said "I just love 4N, Brad, I've tripled my business in the last year as a result."

So when I was mugged by Mr Z with the same franchise, I scratched my head for a second, and then asked a question back:

"Which bit, of you talking to people about your business, isn't working?"

Needless to say Mr Z is no longer a member. Personally I think he'd been mis-sold his franchise, had built up loads of frustration, was getting nowhere with venting to the franchisor and needed to take it out on someone.

Me? Don't worry; I'm a big lad, I can take it.

The point is this. Networking, however you undertake it, is a platform not a guarantee. I recently bought a 'hole digger' from B&Q. Two weeks in and it's not dug a single hole. What a waste of money.

It's called a spade. It's a tool which will rapidly speed up the process, if used correctly.

Mr Z got me thinking; why it is that two people using the same playbook can have completely different experiences from networking?

I pondered and pondered, trying to come up with the answer and no, no luck. Driving along one day, then *wallop*, I'd sussed it. I know why Mr Z failed to win any business where Mr X succeeded. Because no one liked Mr Zzz. Mr Z would come to 4Networking meetings with a face like a slapped backside, miserable, dour and negative.

'Likeability' is always going to attract people to do business with you and the reverse is also true.

There are some networking organisations whose foundations are built on only having one profession within each group. Wonderfully romantic and idyllic networking Utopia that. But a Utopian idea that, in my view, creates a whole load more problems than it solves. I'll get off my soap box/cross now.

Anyway, we took the view with 4Networking to adopt the opposite stance. Have as many people from the same industry as the room can fit. And you know what? It works. You'll often find an 'IT Corner' where all the cyber geeks hang out and communicate in their own special language.

And before I have a revolt, let me ask you a question. Would you go to a trade show if your competitors were in attendance? Would you go to a networking event if your competitors were in attendance? Some would say no way! What's the difference?

What's wrong with a meritocracy?

That's what the real world of business is about, working with and alongside competition. Your ability to adapt and set yourself apart from the crowd. The real world is full of competitors and as soon as you recognise that that is life, the better you will be able to deal with them.

Then one day I broke it right down. Mr Z had never had a chance. He may have had the best product ever but if he never engaged with anyone, they'd never get to know.

I'd like you to think about your best friend, your wife/husband/lover/partner and your best clients. Generally speaking, the process we go through to form an opinion of them is this:

Meet

We make split-second judgments when we meet people. Judge a book by its cover.

Like

You enjoy spending time and being around this person.

Know

Sometimes, when you get to know someone, you no longer like that person and they drop out of your life. Or you move onto the next, most important step...

Trust

This is when the magic happens; "Would you like to come back to my place for coffee". Business, leads and introductions start flowing.

This was never more evident than in a situation at a breakfast meeting in Bicester, near Oxford. Picture the scene. 25 upbeat attendees: all good. Sauntering into the meeting came a visitor with an air of arrogance; the only way to describe him is he was looking for a fight. Not necessarily a physical one, although I always carry my gum shield just in case, but clearly looking for a reason to dislike the group.

So in he swans, hands behind his back, saying yes umm, yes umm, like a *Westworld* cyborg, wired up wrong. I decided to break this cycle of negativity, so armed with a coffee I made a beeline for him, trying my best to engage him in conversation about him and his business. He couldn't wait to tell me how he "bills out at £1000-£1500 a day" and as he "deals with the likes of Shell & BP, the businesses here seem a little 'low rent'."

Now I've seen this type of character before; it's a certain set that I call 'cufflinkers', who I'll talk about more in Chapter 7.

I said, "Geez, you should have made it to Cirencester a few weeks back. We had Sir Alan Sugar speaking."

"Did you really?" he said

"No." I said. "No, come to think of it, it was Weston-Super-Mare." I saw the funny side, even if my new-found friend didn't.

Anyway, he joined the rest of the group and the meeting got underway. Throughout the meeting he'd be looking over his half-moon glasses, sneering at the serfs. I felt like I was back in the magistrate's court for that speeding offence.

As we broke to begin the first of the three appointment rounds, I had my 1-1 with him. As the time to swap partners neared, we closed the meeting off and I asked one of the other members to come over. Bearing in mind I knew the answer to this question, I asked "Neil, who does your brother work for?"

"BP"

"What's his job title?"

"Director of Marketing for the UK"

"Young man, could we have a 1-1?" asked Mr BP/Shell.

"Too late, I'm fully booked and I've got to leave bang on 10," said Neil, brother of Director of Marketing for BP UK.

Had our friend not been so oafish, I'd have asked Neil to join us and said

"Neil, your brother works for BP at director level, doesn't he? Any chance you could have a sit down with Geoff after the meeting as he needs an intro into the organisation."

So what did the snippiness achieve? Nothing, absolutely nothing; it got everyone's backs up and was counter-productive to Geoff's goals.

He was completely missing the point.

By all means sell to the room, but sell through the room also. That means selling yourself and what you do to the people in the room in a way that makes them want to sell you to their contacts.

I urge you not to regard people just in their current job title, but recognise that everyone has far-reaching experience & contacts well outside their current role.

Resist the urge to look at people with pound signs over their heads in terms of what are they worth to you in business today, but look towards cultivating relationships that last well beyond the time it takes for the invoice to clear.

I see so many people looking for quick wins, wanting to come away with wheelbarrows full of work. Networking doesn't work like that. It's about the people and it's about trust.

I treat everyone the same. Really, nothing changes with me, perhaps I'm somewhat autistic in my approach, but everyone deserves a bench line level of respect.

There is no one I hold in higher regard than Colin, the carpet cleaner *www.mchcarpetcleaners.co.uk*. Colin is an absolute legend in 4Networking circles, he's so honest, his prices are far too cheap — really he could charge 30% extra and no one would bat an eyelid. He's up and down the UK network, sharing with us his horrendous albeit hilarious 'on the job' carpet cleaning stories, and everyone just loves him. Everyone universally adores and respects Colin.

Meet, like, know & **TRUST**.

How has honest Colin built that trust over time?

Let's dissect it.

Great prices – too low.

Gives away tips on removing your own carpet stains. I'll never forget; you spill red wine on a carpet, quickly pour white wine on it! Want to know how to get rid of the mixture, use salt. The guy actually tells you how to avoid using him and paying his inexpensive costs.

What!! Let's just rewind that; not only has he got exceptional prices, he tells you how to do it yourself, avoiding the cost of using him.

Legend. A total legend.

So much so he's earned the nickname MIGHTY COLIN HICKS, THE CARPET CLEANER – remember that name, we'll come back to it later.

So with that model, how do you transfer that into how you do things?

There's not a single business on this planet that couldn't learn a lesson or two from our tradesman, Col.

Would you do business with people you don't like?

Would you do business with people you don't know?

Would you do business with people you don't trust?

Of course not, so how do some get it so wrong at networking and expect others to forgo those same checks and instantly give you the mythical wheelbarrow full of work?

Therein lies the secret to encouraging people to refer business to you. You don't need a three day intensive referral workshop in order to "ask for the referral". It's much simpler than that. Get them to meet, like, know & trust you.

I've seen people underestimate our Col. Underestimate him at your peril, because he is an opinion-former and he could deal break your next deal. Not that he would do that maliciously, but by disregarding his influence you could inadvertently kibosh your next big client.

Someone like Colin is brilliant for what I call conversational strategy. He's out there in the houses of other networkers and businesses each and every day, five days a week, whilst being plied with yet more cups of tea, so he'll talk. If you have done the right thing by him and treated him well, he'll talk positively about you, your interests and will actively look out for jobs for you.

What's the downside of being nice to the Mighty Colins of this world? There is none. So the key to any human transaction in networking is first and foremost, being liked. Everyone has value, even if you don't see it right away.

A wise and great friend of mine, Roy Hurley, shared something with me once. Roy said, "Treat people like bank accounts; always ensure you are in the black. Every time you ask someone to do something, this counts as a withdrawal and it will need filling again." Yet so many employers/people continue to draw heavily into the red.

So you have to somehow manage people, from the point of meeting you all the way through to trusting you. It's really not that difficult, unless of course you are a toe-rag.

Accept that not everyone will like you. We're all individuals and all have different personalities.

I used a similar method on day one of my first business and it won me my first three jobs. Hot, warm, cold.

You'll need five pieces of paper for this next belting (that's Manc for very good) exercise.

First piece of paper: write down all the people you know - friends, family, bloke at the shop and so forth.

Then on each of the remaining four pieces of paper write each of these headers:

MEET
LIKE
KNOW
TRUST

And then transfer each person, one by one, to the relevant piece of paper.

Before you concentrate on widening your network, ensure you've deepened your existing one. Spend the time and create the conditions to transform your relationship with contacts to one of mutual trust.

The great thing about networking is that if you do a good job, everyone gets to know about it. And the other great thing about networking is if you do a bad job everyone gets to know about it. It's a business eco-system at work.

TRUST

Trust is the best marketing tool you have. I recognised that early on.

I've experienced business situations where someone has simply thrown away that trust at the very point they have won it. I wonder if these people knew exactly what they were doing - anyway they were found out.

Have you heard the story about the frog and the scorpion?

A frog is on the side of riverbank. The scorpion comes over; the frog is just about to hop off, when the scorpion asks the frog to take him across the river to the other side of the bank on his back. The frog refuses. "You may kill me". And the scorpion says, "No way! If I did that I would surely drown".

The frog couldn't argue with that logic, so he agreed. The scorpion hops on the frog's back and the frog gets halfway across when he feels a searing pain in his back. The scorpion has stung him. As the frog is breathing his last, he asks the scorpion, "Why have you done that? You will surely drown and die now."

"I'm a scorpion," replied the scorpion. "That's what we do. We kill frogs." They both drown.

No more fables, certainly not in this chapter, I promise. But there's a point here, that you are who you are. Don't pretend to be something you are not, in order to win trust. People get found out real fast because you can't keep the mask on forever. So this is why you need to be true to yourself, unless of course you're not a nice person, in which case change those ways.

Sometimes people foolishly forgo the natural stages, jumping straight to trust, based not on liking or knowing someone.

We base our trust on projected telephone number revenues and allow ourselves to be blinded by hope or greed or 'certainty', particularly when someone offers us a deal that is too good to be true.

But you want to believe that you just happen to be in luck this time and that somehow you're special.

Certainty. I believe that's why I've seen sensible, bright, intelligent people rush to the front of seminars, chequebooks in hand, to buy a three day course for £5,000. They've just been sold certainty.

Knowing you're aware of this is not enough. Watch out for

the 'certainty' salespeople. In my world, I encounter this a lot with franchises and MLM (Multi Level Marketing), where due diligence goes out of the window along with trust, as all that is being presented is 'comp plans' and those telephone number revenues.

Beware at networking meetings the HARDCORE Multi Level Marketers aka MLM Zombies,

who never take no for an answer, regardless of how reasonable your questions are. They answer them only by sending you to a website or insisting that you watch a short 25 minute film.

Like Zombies in the films, only a headshot will stop them.

Look, I'm not saying that all franchises and MLMs are scams, no sirree. But there are most certainly some really dodgy ones.

I'll give you an example.

£7k franchise for a chocolate fountain business. You know the things? You see them at weddings etc. For your £7k you get:

1 x chocolate fountain − £1500

1 x apron − £50

1 x training day − covering set up/close down of the kit + marketing your chocolate fountain business.

So, using my calculator, I deduce that the kit equates to about £1550, leaving nearly £6k on the table to learn how to melt some chocolate and stick strawberries onto a 15 centimetre cocktail stick.

Oh please! Come on! Are you really telling me that the 'day's training' is worth £5950?

OK, I'm sure there's a bit more to it than that, but there are people out there who would prefer to pay £7k for £1550 worth of stuff. Why? Because they believe that the excess money is buying certainty, the certainty that it will work.

'Former' friends of mine fell foul of this. I tried desperately to make them see sense, but no. The trust we had was overrun when a smooth-talking salesman rode into town with the promise of riches beyond wildest dreams. Pictures painted in their minds of wonderful houses, fitted kitchens, cars and the obligatory picture of the anchored yacht they wanted; and of course, I couldn't offer them that. All I could offer was advice, support and to be a friend who had their interests at heart.

But the thought of Lamborghinis and swimming pools won out over common sense. So the trust they had with me was thrown out the window in order to fill up the trust bucket of the brigand. Needless to say, the net result was that the company collapsed within three months, with the Directors having lost a load of money and friends in the process.

Titles like 'Director' were being thrown around like confetti.

Everyone was a 'Director' of the company. It was just crazy! Blind goldrush fever and the idea of a ground-floor opportunity. Even to this day, I hear stories about what could have been and it's a total face palm moment.

Trust can't be bought, but it can be won. These scammers prey on greed and promises to make people rich, when in fact they are just stringing them along, making themselves rich until the money runs out. Or alternatively, until someone figures out their game and if you're lucky, tries to warn you.

Fortunately, having seen them operate, I can spot them

a mile away. Hopefully, reading this, you will also be better equipped to slow things down in the event of a 'ground floor opportunity'. Blind faith and certainty.

You can't live your life fearing and not trusting people. My advice is this. As soon as the alarm bells start ringing, hightail out of there.

Equally, I do what I can to trust people in the fastest way possible.

Mark Linton runs a successful exhibition company, *www.corkscrewevents.co.uk*, which covers the whole of the UK. Mark is MD of the Business Growth Show. Somehow we got talking on the phone and hit it off, so we agreed to meet. He came down from Birmingham to our Somerset HQ, where we had just 20 minutes together as an initial meeting, as I needed to drive off somewhere. He came into our boardroom and I explained that we do something at 4N HQ called 'Cards Up Poker'.

Normally in poker, everyone is secretive, hiding their hands and their intent. The aim is to win, with everyone else a loser. With 'Cards Up Poker' it's quite the reverse: we each show our hands, explaining what we are holding and also what we'd really like. The aim is to work out how we can all win. And that's just what happened in that meeting: no terms & conditions, no heads of agreements, just 20 minutes of straight batting. The resulting trading relationship is still going strong, more than two years down the line.

Now, I'd be lying if I said I haven't been stung on a couple of occasions: I have. In lieu of not being able to

inject truth serum into people at
these meetings, you can only go on
what you see, hear and know.

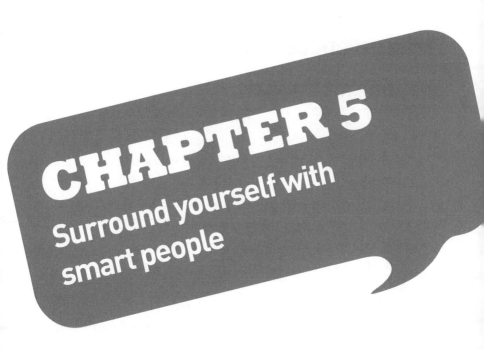

CHAPTER 5
Surround yourself with smart people

A friend of mine, let's call him 'Scouse Allan', because that's what he's called, told me a story of how in the early days of his publishing business back in the early 90s he was totally skint, but he'd borrow money to enable him to go out and do what *he does best*.

I met Allan back in 1999 when I worked at the height of the dotcom boom as a Head of Marketing for UK Online, an internet service provider, and we hit it off big.

In 2001 I ended up working for him as Ad Sales Director at his London-based publishing house. Al taught me so much. At the time I didn't realise he was teaching me anything. But he was.

Like an apprentice I watched how he did things.

What Allan did best was sitting in top London bars & private clubs, spending money, being seen, getting drunk and talking to people. His way of operating was going out with clients and potential clients.

Nearly 10 years on, I continue to use his blueprint on a day-to-day basis. My only amendment is my 'work' waits until the evenings, as I generally travel most days.

Let's be honest, this wasn't real work, this was play, and Allan did it damn well.

The advertising sales came in. I recall a couple of deals worth tens of thousands of pounds made whilst shouting over techno music at a club. Another at 3am in the morning, sitting in a bus stop, pisshed, armed with a bucket of KFC, waiting for a cab. I kid you not.

No Mont Blanc pens, no Ts & Cs. Business on a handshake.

For the first time in my life, I saw something I could be good at. Way before the Facebook and Twitter cyberspace revolution, you could call what we did 'real world social networking'.

Allan had his ear to the ground and everyone knew and loved 'Scouse', including me. He would make things in business happen fast. Someone had a problem, as a friend of Al, he'd make a quick phone call with a "Right, that's sorted, what are you drinking?"

Allan asked. Things happened. He was connected; people wanted to know him. It was self-perpetuating.

He taught me that big fat, bald

headed 16st+ northerners with tattoos can actually do alright in business.

Allan's a smart guy, a millionaire many times over and was best man at my wedding.

I recall one occasion, whilst in a drunken stupor and surrounded by 'clients' at Soho House in London (a big haunt for media luvvies), he shared a story with the group about how he'd recently thrown me into a room full of miserable people (I think he may have used slightly choicer language than that) and related how everyone got 'some'.

'Some' in this case was me. I'd get everyone talking, I'd get everyone buzzing. That was the evening the term 'Brad Grenade' was born.

He didn't realise it at the time, but that throwaway munitions comment stuck: 'Brad Grenading' was how I'd powered 4N in the early days. I'd eulogise, David Koresh (of Waco) style, about the network, bringing an upbeat, high energy 'buzzy' yet inclusive culture to the groups, which still stands to this day.

That ethos is awash throughout the network, meaning I no longer need to perform like a monkey. Although of course I still do, even though I don't *need* to. That's how I roll.

Allan proved to me that business needn't be all pompous and formal to be effective. I was so self-unaware back then it's scary. In fact as recently as late 2008, I didn't recognise how 'different' I am to most people in business.

By surrounding yourself with smart people, you pick up smart things. You have more resources at your fingertips and you find out things about yourself, because smart people help bring out the best in you.

Just as my consultancy business was taking off – no, that's unfair, it never really took off – just as it was stabilising into some sort of solid rhythm, I met Tim Johnson at a sleepy craft/ business show at Bridgwater Town Hall in Somerset.

The show was pretty bad. It was a bit like mixing Crufts with a computer games show, that is, it made no sense.

Anyways, it was £35 for a stand and I could afford it, so I went for it.

So we attended, wifey and I. I still have photos from the event. Nothing really happened in terms of business or leads, but walking around the 'show', I came across another stand and lo and behold, manning it was one of the chapter hit squad who had deflowered me as a networking virgin.

Cue Vietnam-vet-type flashbacks, as I recalled my traumatising first experience of networking.

He murmured something like "Sorry about that, but rules are rules" etc. Sitting next to him chatting was another bloke who was involved in some way with the same business. I was introduced to Tim, went to shake his hand and he offered me his left one, which I thought was a bit strange. He then said "It's a bit shorter, the other one."

Great, he only had one arm, why didn't I notice that? I made an incorrect assumption that he was most likely a former military officer. It was just the way he looked, sounded posh and with one arm, that could all add up to a Forces 'Rupert', an officer.

Isn't it funny how we all do that with people; jump to conclusions, based on how they look, speak and dress.

It was to be my lucky day, again.

As Tim also gave me a *pssst* moment, it was yet again *another* cloak & dagger invite to a different 'networking group', and as luck would have it, they also had business to refer to {insert business category here}.

I took up his invite; this must have been about October 2005 time. I'll always remember, because real work came up and I couldn't make the scheduled meeting and forgot all about it to be honest. About six weeks passed and I received a postcard sized invite complete with a 2nd class stamp, which for some bizarre reason, saving 2p on a stamp continues to amuse me to this day.

I made it this time, rocking up, the meeting was OK steady eddy, but I knew business networking could be so much better.

It must have been just before Christmas, as Tim made an announcement at the end of the meeting about a Christmas drinks get together. My luck held, as I wasn't invited.

After the meeting officially closed, as the single visitor, I was then moved away from the main party into a holding *cell*, whilst I received a hard *sell* to join.

To me it felt like a 'Networking Interrogation'; the closed questions were so loaded, all I could sensibly say was YES.

"Would you like more business?"

"YES"

"Do you think your business would benefit from receiving referrals like you saw being passed at this morning's meeting?"

"YES"

"Would you like to join today and lock out your competition, for just £500?"

"NO THANKS"

I'd had enough for one day and quickly made good my escape.

I'd probably already made up my mind to start my own business network in the New Year, but this was just affirmation that there had to be a better way.

A faster, sharper, leaner, meaner organisation; with members' interests put before those of the network.

After that day, Tim and I stayed in contact and would have regular phone conversations. We seemed to admire something about each other, with respective skills and qualities that eluded each of us.

It really was an odd couple, me running a failing marketing business, Tim failing with his Business Mediation gig. But perhaps together we could help each other.

On one such call, Tim suggested we do something called *quid pro quo*; I genuinely had no idea what he was on about. Searched on the internet: Latin apparently.

Save your bandwidth looking, taking directly from Wikipedia it means "something for something, indicating a more-or-less equal exchange or substitution of goods or services."

So, basically, we helped each other with advice.

This is what you need to be looking for: people and organisations that you can swap services, quid pro quo. Barter your time, it keeps all-important costs down and it works.

Tim was a toff, public school, more recently an MBA in business, talking Latin to a northerner with a council estate background who could barely speak the Queen's English.

Massive cultural differences.

One morning, the postman brought me an invite from a solicitor I'd had dealings with. A *cordial* invite along with a +1 to a rugby club apparently; there was such a thing as a free lunch.

Now I'd arranged to take the 'supportive' wife. Joking aside, she has been and continues to be an absolute angel in keeping the wheels on the house and family unit; and I suppose supporting me through my butterfly net swinging of the past and chasing the next big thing of the future. Someone has had to put up with me during the daft idea years of the previous decade or so.

So going forward in this book, I'll put the 'supportive' bit to bed when referring to Kerry, as the gag's getting tired.

'Funny' whilst it lasted. Thanks for being you, wifey. Love you.

So the stage was set; we'd get a babysitter and Kerry would join me for the day. Two days before the game, I said to her, "Kerry would you mind if I invite and take Tim instead please." She feigned everything was alright, with a "No probs"; I knew she was pissed off and quite rightly, but I said, and this is the gospel truth,

"Don't ask me why, but I just know I need to meet with him."

Do you ever get a hunch in business, something you only know through gut instinct?

It was one of those moments.

I steamroller my own way through on occasion and I never feel good about it, but I always extrapolate stuff out in my head and see the bigger picture, even if others don't. This was one of those occasions. I rang Tim: he accepted.

On the afternoon of the game, I hoped to get there before him, so he wouldn't see what I was driving. I'll always remember that my cunning plan failed, as I drove to the away fans car park instead of home.

Pah, wrong car park. Eventually I found the correct one.

Tim rang me on the mobile and asked, "Was that you that just passed in the Vauxhall?"

"Yeah"

Yes, that's me in the M-reg Omega with the rust on the front driver's side wing. I'd been sussed out at the first hurdle for bullshitting about my current situation, gutted.

Anyway, we went to the game and yet didn't watch a single minute. We spent the time talking, hitting it off; if he'd have been of the fairer sex I might have invited him back to mine for a coffee. Meet, like, know, trust. This was the first time I'd revealed my master plan of Somerset domination to anyone other than 'er indoors.

/cackling and manic rubbing together of hands

I had a one hundred year freehold on a hollow volcano, all I needed now, after all, were the Ninjas with the boiler suits.

"With 4Networking, I'm going to create, within two years, the largest business breakfast network in the South West."

At that time, this meant setting up just over a dozen groups. With hindsight, not really that stretching a target, but it was networking as we knew it back then. Twelve groups in two years from a standing start was unheard of. This was indeed a massive goal.

I had asked for his help; Tim had masses of mental horsepower that would help to provide the support and focus I needed.

Take a moment to think about who you have around you. Who could you approach to help you and your business? Ensure they have complementary skill sets, because there's no point in just doubling up yours.

"If you want to create a *national* network, I'll help," said Tim.

"Really? National? Do you think so?"

"Absolutely, why not?"

"OK, let's do it."

I'm not sure at that point whether Tim really believed we could do it, but suddenly we both had a goal, something to aim for. Business without a goal is akin to playing football in a field with kids, without jumpers for goalposts.

Completely pointless.

Returning to my *"Really? Do you think so?"* comment – it's just nuts! Me, 'Mr Dynamic', doubting myself.

I've not always been like that, you understand. I always had self-belief and so forth, but this has been counterbalanced with a self-imposed working class "Not worthy, I'll get found out" ceiling.

So we shook hands (left ones) and at that moment, Tim Johnson, 44, was appointed Director of Strategy. It would be another 18 months before the shareholdings agreed on that day were allocated.

This was the level of trust.

No shareholder agreements.

We couldn't afford them and we realised in fact that if such an agreement needed to come out of the drawer in which it gathered dust, the thing was over anyways.

The whole concept about doing things differently in business was born that day.

In those early days of 4N I 'cold called' visitors for our groups. I stumbled across a nice bloke, 'Terry', and told him about 4N, and although nice enough, he blew me out. In the nicest possible way, being Terry, but it was a blow-out.

At this stage we had eleven groups; then we opened up a group in Portishead, the twelfth one. I then went through the call list and phoned Terry again, since he only lived 10 minutes away from the venue.

I said "It'll only cost you a tenner."

"OK", he agreed. 35 turned up for that launch.

Terry had a corking 40 seconds, which he still uses it to this day, that's how good it is. It goes like this:

"Terry Cooper, Cooper Bradbury Associates, *www.cooperbradbury.co.uk*, based in Clevedon, covering the whole of the South West, and we're passionate about sales. Your business needs sales. Sales are the lifeblood of any business..."

He's not wrong, I thought, yup that's what we need, more lifeblood. More sales.

After the meeting Terry immediately came up to me asking,

"How do I start a group in Clevedon?"

"Well, you go find a venue and get on with it," I said.

That was about as far as our group launch processes went back then. Some groups worked, some didn't, and some fell over as fast as we put them up.

It transpired that Terry had also dicked about* for just under a year, having recently retired after 30 years of service in a plc, reaching the lofty heights of MD on a main board.

Terry was a serious player and he

was getting bored in retirement, as was his wife Lynn, as she didn't need any help around the house.

So Terry came out of retirement and set up his business, only to find that there is a world of difference between running a one-man-band operation and managing multi-million pound budgets and 700+ staff. Ironically the latter was somewhat easier; remember the lamb cutlet story?

So Terry's group went off like a rocket and so did he. He set the pace of the growth of the network; we then promoted him to an Area Leader role, managing eight groups. This was rapidly followed by a Regional Leader role, which meant managing Area Leaders, which he needed to find. Everything Terry touched turned to gold.

We renamed him Terry Christmas, as with his trademark white beard he looked a bit like Father Christmas and always brought cheer, Christmas or not.

A damn smart operator, he was back doing what he does best: managing teams, making things and sales happen.

We needed Terry as much as he needed us. Enter stage left the third Director in the team. Terry Cooper, 57, Development Director — tasked with developing the UK.

I then met Tamsen Garrie at 4Networking in Cardiff, South Wales, at our first foray into another country. '4Networking International' was born.

"Look, mum! I'm MD of an international business."

Terry had met Tamsen at her first visit to Cardiff 4N a fortnight before; he was taken by her and her approach, so he arranged for us to meet during the following session.

At the meeting, disappointingly, we had only seven people in attendance, a far cry from the 23.7 average across the network as it is today.

As the meeting was brought to a close, cracks began to show in the Group Leader's performance. I assume she felt under some pressure because I was sitting there and we only had a handful of people.

Anyway, she began to cry, before running off to hide in the loos. I immediately stepped forward, picking up the script to close the meeting. "Well, that was a Salvador Dali moment. Oh look, the clock's melting," I said.

That was possibly the most surreal thing ever to happen in the history of a 4Networking meeting, unless you disregard the time when an attendee started choking on a sausage. Fortunately the Group Leader performed a Heimlich manoeuvre before placing him in the recovery position ready for the arrival of the ambulance.

I never once pretended back in those early days that a group of seven people is better because "it's more intimate". Total cobblers.

Honestly, we really didn't know what we were doing in those early days. Don't get it perfect, just get it going. There was no '4Networking Rule Book' back then. It half worked. Which half, we'd work out later.

Tamsen has a background in HR, having worked at Goldman Sachs in London before choosing a different path. She spent four years in Australia training as a clinical psychologist/hypnotherapist; this was her fifth month back in the UK, her third trading as a hypnotherapist.

However, I have since found out that at our first meeting together, she found me "bonkers", yet got me, straightaway. I just didn't realise the sheer passion I have for this thing, therefore I was blissfully unaware of how I came over.

As a total over-enthusiastic nut job, fortunately I'm slightly more temperate than I used to be.

Like Terry before her, Tamsen trail-blazed, giving first, never asking for anything in return.

Operations Assistant, Group Leader, Area Leader...

The speed at which Tamsen set up 4N South Wales was unheard of, thirteen rocking groups in just short of three months! Networking the world over had never seen growth like that. We'd seen the future of what 4N could be across the UK.

We thought we only needed three Directors, until we met Tam. She is that good.

So, 4 Directors, 4Networking, sounds about right. Game on.

Network Director for the whole of the UK, that's a real Director by the way, that is, on the 4N board, which should not be confused with an aspiration title bandied around in other circles.

Tam provides support, advice and most importantly, has found the time to put in place the processes and stuff needed to take us from a regional to a national operation.

She's also the Mother Hen of the team, banging our heads together on the odd occasion when we (generally Tim and I) lock horns.

Each of the other three Directors got 'Bradded'; it's now an official term in the lexicon of 4Networking. Here's the description of 'Bradding' from our pocket guide to networking:

"An experience, not necessarily pleasurable or painful, of being persuaded to do something by 4N Managing Director, Brad Burton."

What a story: these people all came together from three different generations, with so many random factors. Think about that. The answer to your business success and growth may well be right under your nose.

Hopefully, having read this chapter, you can see the value in surrounding yourself with people much smarter than yourself.

You have to be willing to take a chance on people, as they have with you. Each of these people supported me when I had nothing to give, bar certainty! In this case, certainty that I'd give it my best shot to make 4N a rip-roaring success.

Without getting nominated for a Gwyneth Paltrow award, I'd like to thank all those who supported me and to take this opportunity to recognise you for making a difference to me.

/wipes tear

You know how much I like my lists? Why not start one which covers your skills? What you are really great at? Below that list, another list of what you are not so great at – those skills you are lacking, but which are needed to push your business.

You'll find the person you are looking for and need, who may well be needing and looking for you. Then go and hunt down people who can work with you on a *quid pro quo* basis and create yourself a virtual company. Collective strength and shared resource wins every time.

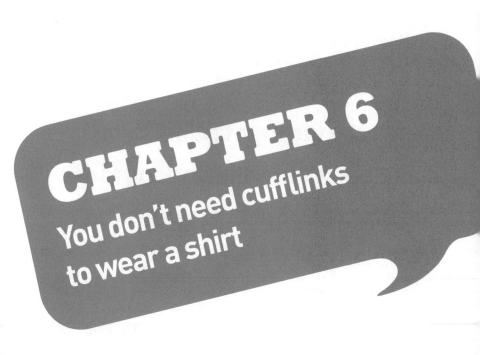

CHAPTER 6
You don't need cufflinks to wear a shirt

S o, I paid the £15 door fee at an evening networking event. The best way to describe it was that it was like a school disco. Everyone around the outside of the room, nervous, scared to make a move, scared to dance.

How do I know this?

Because I was one of them: petrified.

You pay your money and then you're left to your own devices. We've all been to networking events like this. Referred to as 'open networking', it's hardcore, really hardcore. You have to move right out of your comfort zone or go mob-handed to succeed.

Succeeding, in these environments, is the equivalent of placing 52 playing cards face down and trying to match up pairs, card by card. You'll eventually find what you are looking for, but it's hardly a science.

I blame my mum. "Don't talk to strangers," she said.

Thirty or so years on, I have no option. Welcome to open networking. Unfacilitated, hard work, the networking equivalent of the jungle, where the strong survive and the weak are fodder.

These are the events where you come across the 'networking tom cat', spraying out business cards like a tom cat's pee!

Like so many others, you enter the room looking like a lost child searching for its parents, or in this instance for someone you recognise. If you could just find someone you know, that would be sanctuary and you'd feel safe.

Failing that, the old 'pretend to be talking on a mobile phone' or 'picking up emails from the BlackBerry' is a good trick.

As the waitress saunters past with yet another tray of white wine, another 'lost child' asks "Is that a Chablis?"

Who gives a shit?

We're not here for Chablis or vol-au-vents (I did some research – 'vol-au-vent', loosely translated from French, means 'windblown' to describe their lightness – you couldn't make it up...)

Anyway, back to the story. For some of us, this event was akin to some bizarre business networking/Benny Hill hybrid. All the 'lost child' networkers, ie those who had arrived alone, spent half the evening chasing the girl with the meat samosas, whilst the remainder pretended to be on the phone.

There's an art to succeeding at this kind of networking, there really is, but it bores me senseless.

Networking shouldn't be hard work and neither should business.

My advice is to steer clear from open networking as a primary networking option, unless of course you are mob-handed, in which case you have safety in numbers.

So there I am, nervy as hell, furtively looking around, glued to the wall with fear, sipping my white wine, plate loaded with fire-roasted aubergine bruschettas, not really knowing what to do next.

Have you ever been in this situation?

I eventually plucked up the courage to think:

"*Sod this!* I paid £15; I need to get some value out of this event. So I'll do my countdown from 10 routine, then I'll go."

10, 9, 8, 7, 6, 5, 4, 3, 2, 1

Nope, I'll sip some more wine.

It's just so tough. What a lottery.

Everyone on their best behaviour, 'shields up', Star Trek stylee. Again, *"I'll try 10, 9, 8, 7, 6, 5, 4, 3, 2, 1, and this time I'll go for it!"*

I head towards what's known in 'expert networking circles' as a 'closed two'.

Impressive, eh?

Hand extended, "Hi guys! Can I jump in?"

Introducing myself, we get talking. See? That wasn't so bad after all. About two minutes into the generalities, one of them (let's call him 'Blokey A') starts talking about how he's just bought the new Range Rover *Sport*. Apparently it has twenty inch 'anthracite coated' wheels as standard and Blokey A has paid extra to have some sort of limited edition leather piping on the interior.

In response, the other bloke (Blokey B) turns to tell us about his vehicle.

Uh oh. We've got ourselves sucked into a *bullshit arms race*.

Gorbachev and Reagan had nothing on this. The proliferation of ICBMs was a mere bagatelle compared to the scene unfolding.

We reach *Defcon 2*, as Blokey B fires back his first salvo. This time it's a warhead primed with an elaborate and convoluted story about how his friend works at BMW Gmbh, and how he managed to get pushed up the waiting list for the new 5 Series *M-Sport*.

Now it was my turn. I chose to enter a metaphorical nuclear bunker in my own head, merely commenting on the *delicious* aubergine bruschettas. I couldn't very well tell them that I had walked for ten minutes to get here to avoid the embarrassment of anyone seeing me exit my chariot, which was not so much *M5* (BMW), more *M-reg* (Vauxhall Omega)...

Parking as close to the wall as possible to hide the rust on the wing was bad enough; getting out the passenger side was even worse.

I felt pretty inadequate; I must be failing in business, as it seemed that, unlike my newly found networking chums, I didn't have those trappings of success.

Cufflinking

This is a term I've coined, and love using, when referring to the "things you find yourself doing or saying just to conform when in a business environment."

One of my favourite business networking/self-employment

experts is a guy called Stefan Thomas of No Red Braces (*www. norebraces.co.uk*), who has shared his experiences of this and how it has affected him.

"I have spent loads of my time in business believing everyone else was more successful than me. This is mainly because they were telling me so. Some of them have since gone bust, so they were obviously much better actors than me.

"My first experience of business networking was with everyone in the room showing off how successful they were. Maybe men just aren't great at admitting their failings, the bits they need help with, and as a result they keep telling everyone what great business people they are, even in the face of red letters piling up and repo-men parked outside."

So it appears I'm not alone.

Cufflinking seems to get everywhere, so as a start-up business, if you allow it to, it could really take the wind out of your sails and your sales.

Like Stefan, I found it disconcerting.

In this situation, the reason we'd got onto cars had been largely down to the 'lottery balls' approach at these gigs of who I'd ended up speaking to. This randomness can create really bad matches in terms of people and the net result, more often than not, is that you end up talking to people about nothing of real common interest.

It is, however, one rung up from standing against the wall

eating 'Leek and wild mushroom vol-au-vents with watercress coulis' (I just found that on the internet).

That's not a contradiction. As I've mentioned before, everyone has value, of course they do, but the school disco environment isn't the productive way to get the best out of networking and may encourage the cufflinking we've talked about.

Of course, there is always the story about how XX met someone and got a £10,000,000 contract to build a space shuttle. But that's down to lottery networking rather than science. I do accept, though, that school disco networking is better than no networking.

I've been guilty of minor cufflinking myself. I didn't admit to the car. Why?

Because I was embarrassed. That's called 'complicit cufflinking'.

Even though I was born & bred in Manchester, I used to put on a daft posh voice when undertaking presentations. Now I'm not suggesting for a minute I should sound like Frank from *Shameless* or Liam Gallagher, but equally I shouldn't *pretend* to sound like Ralph Fiennes. *Cufflinking*!

Back in 2004, just before I started working for myself, I was working at a firm in London, alongside a sales team. The sales manager came in one day with a double Windsor knot tie – the kind you'd most likely see Chris Eubank wearing. Next thing, the entire sales team starts wearing them. Who am I to argue? Enter Brad stage right, looking like something straight out of *The Apprentice*. Cufflinking.

Granted, I never went as far as the red braces, pink socks thing.

Conforming kills creativity and yet sometimes it's easier to conform than not to conform.

Cufflinks are a big thing for me. I should take this opportunity to point out that I have nothing against cufflinks themselves. Hey, I even wore them at my wedding; but that whole thing about power dressing? It's gone.

The 80s can take back their red braces. Dress for business how you feel comfortable dressing.

Behave in business how you feel comfortable behaving.

So many times, within minutes of meeting someone, I'm asked, "What is your exit strategy?" *Cufflinks*. It's the kind of thing you hear said when someone doesn't know what to say.

Here's an absolute peach, which I'm sure you've come across: "I **NEED** BIGGER BUSINESSES!"

Cufflinks.

No you don't. You need to make your mortgage payments.

This is a sure-fire sign of a cufflinker. In a previous chapter you had your first introduction into Mr Bills-out-at-£1500-a-day. Here's another story that demonstrates how this behaviour works counter to your business goals.

I met someone at a 4Networking event who was hyping up his business no end. "Oh, I work with Fortune 500 companies; my customers are people like Microsoft and IBM blah blah blah."

He told me in a 1-2-1 that he was "only interested in £1m+ businesses and that means 4Networking wouldn't be any good for me." Because of his £1m+ rule, of course he didn't get any business from the room, nor did he join, nor did he get the whole concept of selling 'through the room'.

What's to 'get'? Every person in a room knows people; they each know more people. A real-life Twitter.

A while later he contacted me for advice because he had commissioned a logo from one of those '20 logo designs for

$200' sites and now wanted some 'amends', for which he was being quoted $80 extra; something, it turns out, Mr. Fortune-500-Seeker couldn't afford.

I spoke to him recently and it appears he is going through a "lean period" and "has nothing on at all". Work wise, that is.

Sitting in a boxroom wearing a Savile Row suit, is still sitting in a boxroom.

The 'cufflink gamble' didn't pay off for him.

If he hadn't had his head so far up his own backside he might have engaged the people in that room; and many other networking rooms full of people he perhaps could have done business with. Granted, they might not have been Fortune 500, but surely that has to be better than UB40.

So why do people behave like this? Have a think for a moment as to what those reasons could be.

I needed to get speak to someone who had done the corporate thing and done it well. Looking through my phone, I came up with the number of sales expert Gill Bray of Business Hat, *www.businesshat.co.uk*. She would be just perfect to give me the inside track, as she had worked within pharmaceutical giants for over 30 years before leaving to start her own sales consultancy. It doesn't get any cufflinkier than that!

If anyone could share insights from inside corporate to now outside corporate, it was Gill.

Boy, was I right! What she shared with me on our call was eye-opening. I'll let her explain:

"My experience has been in the context of helping business consultants to get themselves to market and I have found that they have become stuck mentally in a past role in which they were successful or had high status.

So, it seems to make perfect sense to try to be that same person outside, to behave in the same way and use the same language in order to market themselves.

The point they miss is that those exact roles and the language that goes with them, are largely irrelevant in SME-land.

The thing that gets in the way of helping them move on is that they usually haven't been able to sit down with someone to work out what they achieved in their previous role, and to see what value the abilities and experience used for that success will have in their new SME market.

The worst part is that they don't actually believe in their own marketing, when you get below the surface. Nevertheless they believe in their ability to market themselves to others, based on past glories.

Therefore, underneath all the jargon and flimflam is usually a very, very scared and unconfident person.

What I love doing is being able to get rid of all the old flaky paint and let them see what still shines underneath, so that they can be genuinely confident about whatever it is they have achieved, build on it, and shout about it. It's just basic sales management stuff really."

The lesson here is to find out what people achieved in their roles, not just what the titles of the roles or the tasks were.

Ignore the "responsible for"; "managed 1200 people successfully"; "working in a market-leading way". Instead, focus on "What did you *achieve?*" Either you alone or what was your specific contribution to a team's result.

When you find out the last bit, you can see what you achieved and what is relevant and saleable to your current market. Build on that.

OK, it's a bit broad brush, but we talked previously about how in corporate they rarely embrace entrepreneurial spirit. The contradiction is that they train people to be entrepreneurial, because it looks and feels good, but entrepreneurship is completely useless in most corporates – they don't need it!

They need people who will help the blunt-nosed tanker to stay on course and the crew to buckle down. So you end up with all these great 'entrepreneurial leaders' being useless, with sod-all management skill or knowledge.

It's a case of "maintain the status quo, play the game". Self-employment is 100% different.

Therein lies the danger.

When someone transitions out of corporate they are stuck in 'corporate speak' and 'cufflinking'.

The reality is that when you first start a business you have to be more like a market trader, selling what you can, when you can, how you can.

This isn't a finger-pointing exercise, as I've been guilty of cufflinking myself, but having come out my 'phase', I think it's fair to say I am more effective as a business person and my relationships are stronger as a result of ditching cufflinks.

Over the last few years, I've met many PR (Public Relations) people, most of whom make a living out of cufflinking.

PR is much simpler than you'll be led to believe. Really it's as simple as emailing a press release and then picking up the phone to speak with a journalist who writes for your target publication.

Journalists are lazy...well, some of them are. I know; I used to be one.

If you can make their job easier, surely that has to be a good thing.

Send them a press release and give them the story. If it's a case of cutting and pasting a sensible pre-written story and getting off to the pub instead of working in the office for an extra hour thinking out a story... well, which would you do if you were in their shoes?

According to some (possibly PR people), PR has three times the impact of advertising. There are experts all over the place, but don't be sold on PR on the basis that it's a dark art. It's a whole lot simpler than that.

If you've got a good story, for the right publication, guess what? It'll be printed.

The point is that decent PR people are worth their weight in gold but I've encountered a lot of wafflers in recent years, who convolute and cufflink the whole process, in an attempt to make you believe it really is a dark art and therefore worth paying through the nose for.

If you have no story, you have no chance.

Great story, great chance!

I'll leave you with a story which came to my attention whilst on my mission to shine a light under as many rocks and onto as many pontificators (being cruel in order to be kind) as I could.

The person who shared this story wishes to remain anonymous. Fair do's.

"I have an accountancy contact who has the most qualifications I've ever seen on a business card, some I'm sure purchased from dubious American colleges and who is always on about his jet-setting lifestyle.

I know his wife, who is independently wealthy and who

has had to bail him out twice. That doesn't stop the bullshit and he has become a figure of ridicule in the community. In a wind-up we convinced him he needed to a get a 'CDM, plus bar' to complete his collection of qualifications. He hasn't cottoned on yet that CDM stands for 'Cadbury's *Dairy Milk*.'"

This is not an isolated example. We must, collectively, help these people to recognise that this sort of approach is doomed to failure. The more honest we can be in business, using trust and transparency, is the key to unlocking long and fruitful relation-ships; not *John Rocha* loafers and stripy *Pierre Cardin* socks.

This chapter has been really a bit of fun, but like everything in this book, it has an underlying theme and a common-sense message which hopefully rings true.

However you behave, just remember to be true to yourself.

So the next time you're asked to share your exit strategy by a member of the bruschetta brigade at a school disco, respond with a

"Well, that depends on our brand-robust metrics; our ability to monetize one-to-one partnerships whilst unleashing seamless architectures to e-enable B2C relationships. If, and it's a big if, that happens, then maybe we'll evolve convergence to the point where an exit is at optimum visionary crux to en-sure an ROI."

CHAPTER 7
Shit happens. Get used to it

"The computer says 'no'," the bank manager told me in response to my overdraft request.

You may have heard it too. The money was needed in my early days to get me through the next few months of trading. All I needed was that little push to the next stage and things would have been alright. As it happens I didn't get the overdraft and yet I'm still here. It's surprising how resourceful and resilient you become when faced with no other options.

We've been through the virtual collapse of the global banking system, with banks going to the wall. The ones that haven't are being propped up by the government to the tune of billions of your taxpayer pounds. Your money is being used to prop up banks, and by proxy, justify fat cats. Fat cattery. Yet when you go to the bank for a loan for your small business you get "the computer really does say 'no'."

Guess what? Shit happens. Get used to it.

Calls are being made each and every day that affect us massively, yet you and I have no control over them. The only thing throughout your life over which you really do have control is your actions, and to a lesser extent, your thoughts.

It might make no sense, but I'm telling you that a recession is a good thing.

Trust me. I'm a guru.

Recession forces change. Lazy business practices die out (unless propped up); crap business models are replaced with better ones.

Look at Woolworths. OK, granted, 4,000 people or so have lost their jobs and that's never a good thing. But remember, I've also signed on the dole and lived on benefits. Being on the dole is a great grounding and the resulting adversity can force you to reassess everything you once knew and prepare you for a new future.

It's all very well standing outside Woollies, being interviewed by Sky News and crying over how another retail institution has fallen, but hold back your crocodile tears for one second...

Honestly, when was the last time you really shopped there, other than for sweets? I recall trying to and failing to buy Frankie Goes to Hollywood's *Relax*, on 7" picture disc, back in October '83.

Thinking about Woollies reminded me of a story. I don't know about you, but Pick n' Mix, for some bizarre reason, I used to go and think, "OK, 89p for 100 grams. What I'll do is try one and if I like it, I'll buy some."

So I'd open the Perspex flap and quickly *try* a chocolate Brazil.

Never bought a quarter. Ever.

Flawed model. I relabelled it 'Nick n' Mix.'

Guess what? Woolworths.co.uk rises from the ashes, comes back online. 'Pick n' Mix' is alive and well and has evolved into a 'new & improved' business model which means brigands like me can't have away one foot gummy snakes without paying. That has to be a good thing.

A friend of mine who shall remain nameless is a freelance creative designer of the highest order; his career has seen him at some of the top UK ad agencies. I know he's worked on top end accounts, with silly-priced 'brand designs'.

I asked him,

"What's the difference between a £1000 logo and a 25 grand one?" He said, "Honestly? £24,000 worth of bullshit."

More expensive isn't always better; I've often made that mistake whilst eyeing up a restaurant menu.

One of the creative agencies he worked for regularly has just gone into receivership. The rules of the game have changed. Ivory towers & frosted glass offices are great, but a couple of months of low/no sales and guess what? You're still paying for them.

From our conversations it appears to me that in the current climate, budgets are being slashed and expenditure is being looked at more closely. You need to be able to justify your offering and so I can see more companies taking the £1k brand option.

The same guy also told me that the same firm charged £37 to 'print' a pdf document. 'Print' in this case, was pressing two keys, 'control' & 'P'. THIRTY SEVEN POUNDS!! How lazy must they be to not check invoices? Or stupid, to accept it as a legitimate charge. Too much money makes businesses stupid and lazy.

Businesses which have previously survived on over-inflated costs or relied on formerly cash-rich but lazy and stupid clients will struggle to survive. Their clients now have no option other than to look closely at costs and once they begin asking "Why the hell are we paying £37 for a one minute job?", the cat will be out of the bag. These 'evil' businesses will begin to lose contracts to more open, fair, transparent business practices.

That has to be a good thing.

Businesses are having to get savvier with their buying, savvier with their spending. I know I am. Look at the telltale signs. Your suppliers, or worse still, you, are serving up BS in pursuit of the sale. If you're still relying on that approach, you could be walking your business towards oblivion.

Recently, I had a visit from a salesperson flogging advertising in some business magazine. Into the office she came and began her pitch.

I asked a straight question: "If I spend the £1,500 you are asking per month, how much income will it generate?"

Without any hesitation she said, "It will generate at least twice as much."

"Fantastic!" I said.

I wanted to be dead certain that we were on the same page and asked for clarification.

"Do you honestly believe it'll do double?"

"Absolutely, maybe even triple," she said.

I sat forward, interested. At this point she could smell blood.

"OK," I proposed, "so on that basis how about you give me the first advert for free and if we get the results as you claim, a 100% return, I'll book every month for the year?"

I guess the smell of blood quickly evaporated.

"Well we can't do it like that, because blah blah blah"… mumble.

I was offering to place £18,000 worth of advertising on the understanding that her product did what *she told me* it would. Is that so unreasonable? Whatever, she wasn't taking me up on the offer for some reason.

How can I be expected to have confidence in a product when the person selling it me doesn't? You can't have it both ways.

The above is a canny trick; you may want to lift and use it to disarm hardcore sales people selling advertising. But hang about! In this climate, in fact in any climate, it's a fair play.

Business people are getting savvier. In the past, there might have been a point when I would have agreed with her, but nah, right now, more than ever, you need to review how you are selling your goods and services. Look at what you are offering and ask yourself:

"Do I *really believe* in what I'm selling?"

If the answer to that question is "no", then sell something else. Something you *do* believe in.

Before you start making outrageous and unsubstantiated

claims about your product or services to me, or indeed to any potential clients, make sure that if you are challenged, you can back them up.

Surely it was actually worth a punt to give me the first ad free, had the service worked as was suggested? They'd have had a new client and £18,000 extra on their top line.

But once again "the computer said 'no'". I believe this is a stock phrase used at the end of a transaction which is doomed to fail because the reality, when calculated, doesn't match the story.

Consider creating deals and offers to which people cannot say no. I often get approached with 'no brainers' and, guess what? I go for them.

If you believe in what you punt, then shared risk and shared reward deals are the way forward.

In retail, they use a 'sale or return' model. I place my product in your store; if it sells you pay me; if it doesn't you return it, no quibbles.

These types of deals are much more palatable to the buyer. There is little or no risk attached to them, and, if they work out, they are much more profitable to the seller, as they have increased margins.

Come up with a sale or return approach for your products and services and watch them fly!

Coming through this recession, the world will have changed, hopefully forever. Let's hope we've seen the back of that obscene hardcore capitalism. I say "hopefully", as there are signs of the bonus culture returning.

More and more companies will be choosing the £1,000 logo design, with the excess £24,000 still on the table for the brand builder, but he'll have to develop real reasons to invoice for it.

Recessions force a redress of the balance, the normalisation of markets.

Putting common sense back into business, with less waste.

At this time, more and more people are being asked to "take a seat in the office". I've certainly been there. You know the conversation. An HR manager pretending to be posh and saying, "Not great news I'm afraid, Brad, but with the recession biting {insert any old pseudo-plausible cobblers here}, we're going to have to let you go. But don't worry; we'll pay you until the end of the month."

Fantastic! 11 days of pay. Just awesome, the wife will be delighted.

Being made redundant, as in "no longer needed" does something to you well beyond the necessity to find another job. Your psyche takes a wallop and it shakes your confidence to your boots.

Stefan Thomas, *www.noredbraces.co.uk*, is back and this is what he has to say on the subject of employment:

"Being employed is just like being self-employed but with only one client.

"I've got lots of clients, so a lot of them would have to sack me before things became desperate. Being employed, one person sacks you and that's your income gone. Sorry to break it to you. Being self-employed is more secure. This is based on my experience of both."

See, there's this fallacy that having a full-time job means stability. My wife used to say, "You know where you stand and how much you are getting paid each month."

That may once have been the case, but all that changed

with the collapse of Lehman Brothers, the banking institution. Even the Bollinger Boys were asked to clear their desks.

Welcome to the crazy world of imploding hardcore capitalism. However, if you are rowing your own boat, you're in much better control over what happens to you and when.

Recession and 'the downturn' is being used as a smokescreen for piss-poor management.

In the last five years of business I have asked myself at least five times if I can carry on; and there was no recession during that time. You can allow yourself to be consumed by the media. It can be quite easy to convince yourself that you are failing as a result of the economic slowdown.

Answer this honestly. If you hadn't listened to the media, not read the papers and news websites, would you say we've experienced a recession? No? Only about 10% of people at my seminars say that it's had an impact. We've been bundled into it. Look, if you're in finance or the car game or associated industries, you've clearly been affected.

Of course the country's in a mess! I'm not that stupid and neither are you. But there is no advantage in being told so each and every morning. So PLEASE STOP listening to Radio 4 in the morning! It kills your productivity and stifles your entrepreneurial spirit. I tried life without it for a week and guess what? The world still turns and my life is no worse as a result of NOT hearing about more people being killed in wars around the world or the financial markets taking yet another tumble.

Driving to a breakfast meeting at 7am, a week or so after I abstained from John Humphries, I thought I'd tune in again, registering where my head space was at before I switched the radio on.

Answer to that?

Chipper, buoyant and upbeat.

I switched on and listened for 30 minutes, before turning it off at 7.30am, feeling down, sombre and deflated. I felt like doing a Kurt Cobain and topping myself. I've come to the conclusion that the obvious benefits of not listening far outweigh the benefits of 'informed' listening to negative things we have no control over.

The media will stop talking about recession when we stop being interested in recession.

There will be winners and losers in this whole chapter of events; be a winner, by adapting to what people want instead of what you think they want.

We keep on adapting. Recently we introduced a new six-month rolling *4Loyalty* membership. This means that instead of an annual membership of £490, members can renew for £245 every 6 months.

Avoid changing your prices but by all means change your payment terms.

In these times, you may find some invoices start to get paid slower, if at all. Go for 50% upfront deposits from all your clients. My original bank manager said he'd never heard of such a thing and that I'd likely lose prospective clients.

I knew no better, it was my first month of self-employment. I ignored him and went for it.

Guess what? Everyone paid; how good was that? Sometimes, the way things have always been done shouldn't be the way things continue to be done. Give it a go. Not once did I lose a job, not once did I not get that deposit. It's great for cash flow and can be the difference between success and failure, between eating or not!

You want to know the irony of this recession in each of the last six months? They have been record beating month-on-month, smashing to bits previous ones in terms of new members joining 4Networking.

The point is that, as SMEs, we're in a perfect place right now to go "bollocks to this", get smart, increase sales, shave costs and make a difference.

Even when you get it right, you can get it wrong.

Michael Goody, *www.Coloursells.co.uk*, shares with us a story which illustrates the point beautifully:

"I used to have a nice little takeaway burger & pizza business in Tewkesbury. After six years of good business, suddenly a competitor opened up virtually opposite my shop – and then about a month later, another one opened up next door.

Result? Three of us sharing what I was taking before they opened.

Went from 'fast food' to 'slow food' in six weeks. There was no way could I have foreseen that happening.

Took a hell of a job to sell the business before moving on – went off to the USA and created havoc in the printing industry before coming back to Blighty to do the same."

Third parties can change the destination of your life pretty much overnight; remember when internet cafes popped up all over the UK? The future...

Mobility and the proliferation of easily accessible web connections changed all that.

Paul Norman is back. What I haven't mentioned previously is his corporate credentials. In danger of sounding cufflinky here goes...

Former Director of Corporate Strategy at Summit Auto Group, which is part of the Sumitomo Corporation of Japan. Turnover in billions.

One of his claims to fame/shame was that he was involved with British car manufacturer Rover; if anyone knows that "shit happens", it's our Paul.

When I shared with him the title of this chapter he laughed and said:

"It's true. It's vital to success that you do not expect a straight road, a world free of broken stuff and a home run every go. Things break. They wear out. Stuff goes wrong. Plans don't work out. Recessions happen. People naff off without paying their bills. Staff leave. Contractors let you down.

This is reality. It is the backdrop to business and to life but it is the backdrop to success too. Because when things break, you fix them. When they wear out, you replace them or manage another way.

When stuff goes wrong, you change tack and learn. When plans don't work out, you modify and adapt...It was just a plan, anyway.

When recession happens you trim costs, market more innovatively, change your product. You can't sell sun hats on a rainy day so learn to sell umbrellas. When people don't pay, find a way of getting them to pay or cut your losses. Never deal with them again. When staff leave, hire new people; there are millions out there, or do without them. When contractors let you down, work with them to succeed, or reassign the work, and so on.

The common theme, through all this: never be defeated. Learn. Learn. Learn."

In Chapter 5 I mentioned surround yourself with smart people; Paul's one of those people I like surrounding me.

Back in the early days of 4Networking, when we had just three groups or so, we gained a member called John Raine, the Managing Director of IT firm, Tarka Consulting *www.tarkaconsulting.com*.

Big John has a corking sense of humour; I recall on his 65th birthday he shared a profound thought with me: "65 is a difficult age: too young to be a dirty old man and too old to be a toy boy."

During a conversation with him after he reached 'retirement' I said:

"John, you have two options at your age. One, get yourself an orange B&Q apron or two, become a 4Networking Area Leader."

So our first Area Leader was born.

The reason I mention our John is that he had faith in me when this thing was nothing. No books, no big hall speaking seminars, no national network. All I had to offer was a vision. Nearly four years on, John's been promoted again and now manages one of the most effective 4N regions in the UK. One door closes, another opens.

In those early days, someone approached me to become our second Area Leader.

We spent lots of our, at that time, limited money and energy, training this person, who at the earliest opportunity, two weeks after the training, stole our ideas, stole our innovations and 'Othelloed' the members and basically took the group and members over.

In the last three years this Judas's *Flawed Networking* has grown to just five groups, whilst 4Networking is now 200+, with the same resource. You can copy a format to try making a quick buck, that's easy. But what you can never copy is a vision which will make a long-term difference.

Getting ripped off is a nasty drawing pin in that arse. But shit happens, get used to it.

I've just received a call from the MD of a company whom I first met two years or so ago at a trade show at the NEC. Back then this MD was dismissive and arrogant about 4Networking. Fast forward to the present day, he really wants to "work together" with 4Networking.

Not interested; I had great pleasure in being equally dismissive and arrogant.

Anyone can back a winning horse.

On that basis, look to see who you can back today. Back someone who needs your help, someone to whom you can make a positive and real difference.

We've lost our website three times; on each occasion, as a business we could have been ruined. But we didn't panic; when the boat began to sink, we STOPPED.

We took stock, came up with a plan and carried on. Yes it was hairy and unpleasant, but look: we're still here. There's still a long way to go when the shit starts hitting the fan.

Although shit does indeed happen, it's at these volatile times when you establish who your fair weather friends are and those who, when faced with the option of quitting your corner in the dark days, choose not to.

The primary cause of unhappiness is never the situation you are in, but your thoughts about it. So keep the faith that "tomorrow's a brighter day".

Live it.

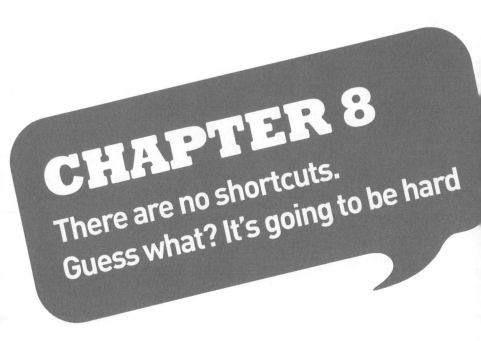

CHAPTER 8

There are no shortcuts.
Guess what? It's going to be hard

S itting there on your stool, bloodied, you've just had a seriously bad round. Knocked down, you barely got to your feet on the nine of a count to ten.

Dejected, no heart to go on and then *"DING DING!"*

No option, you have to go on.

You are now standing up, the stool that provided solace and respite between rounds is no longer there, having been taken away by the very same corner team that supported you for the last minute.

It's time to bite on your gum shield and come out swinging for one more round.

The above could be taken straight from a *Rocky* movie, but it's not. It's a metaphor for self-employment during those formative years.

There are no shortcuts in business; you will go through stages of self-doubt, low sales, in fact NO sales, all garnished by the dark clouds of depression which follow you about.

You are not doing anything wrong. That's how it is.

Whilst running my businesses, there have been numerous occasions when I wondered if I had the testicular fortitude to go on. At least four times I thought about quitting and going back reluctantly to the corporate world. It's only recently, after around five years of running a business, that, sat in the garden one evening, Kerry turned to me and said she's glad I didn't call it a day and "go get a proper job" as she'd suggested. Finally... finally, after five long years...vindication.

I mentioned earlier in the book about gaining wins where you can. That's right! Pat yourself on the back for getting that appointment, for making that cold call, for winning that piece of business. You deserve it. Just when you think you get a break-through moment, just as you think you have reached the summit, you see you have a whole lot further to go.

Cash flow continues to be up and down like a bride's nightie. Yet in my first year, I thought 'cash flow' was a myth and that once you reached a certain size of business, it's no longer an issue.

How naive!

You may be laughing at that statement, but genuinely I didn't know. I think veteran rapper Biggie Smalls summed it up in his seminal track *Mo' Money, Mo' Problems*.

However, he then went on to say something about bitches and drive-by shootings, not really sure how relevant that bit is in a business book. But he got the first bit right or did he?

Mo' Money, Mo' Problems or *No Money, Mo' Problems*? Either way, you have problems.

No money. Self doubt, stress, immense pressure, welcome

to those first years of self-employment.

You are not doing anything wrong. That's how it is.

Oscillation of the workflow (and hence cash flow) of a small business in four stages:

1. Look for business   ☺
2. Hurrah, we've just won a job!   ☺
3. Fulfil the job.   ☺
4. Oh no, we've got no work.   ☹

Repeat step 1.

You only get paid for stage 3. I think I've made my point.

Sadly, from my own experience, in those early days you are so keen on getting business, you don't do the checks you perhaps should. Meaning even if you invoice, it doesn't necessarily follow that you are going to get paid.

Yet this is what I signed up for; and if you are self-employed, this is what you signed up for too. A safe, regular salary in a corporate just wasn't for you and me. That's why we gave it up.

Getting cash flow under control begins with keeping expenditure under control, but given you can't relight a firework, aim to get it right first time.

Get the best you can afford, or in my case, couldn't afford. I have to hold my hand up and say I made some gambles, some business purchasing decisions based on what I think I could sell to cover the costs. After all, I had a 28-day account. Hairy times indeed. Sailed close to the wind on numerous occasions, but guess what? I'm still here.

When will cash flow go into the black? Only you can gauge that. Although it's tempting to not spend on marketing, networking, entertaining (being seen), be aware that you are walking yourself down. You need to have a decent website, brochure, card etc. *Spend wisely.* That's the key.

The next smart move you can make is to use subcontractors. Working with subcontractors is an essential tool to get yourself out of the repetitive boom/bust trap of winning and fulfilling work. You can't do your entire marketing, bookkeeping, invoicing, post room *and* deliver your core business, all by yourself.

Finding decent 'grubby subbies' is a tough gig. At least it was when I started back in 2005. But when faced with a massive resource pool like 4N, it's just not the big deal it used to be.

Talking about those early days, one of the essential purchases I made was one of those telephone answering services, about £35 a month which I could ill-afford.

"Fake it 'til you make it", up to a point.

Little white lies are OK. Cufflinking sucks.

I recognised that if I was going to be out there meeting clients and doing appointments that a 1571 BT answering service wouldn't cut it. To give off being a competent professional operation in business, perception *is* reality.

So I appointed one and so should you. It gives you peace of mind that your calls are being handled correctly whilst you are plugging away on a daily basis.

I'll be honest with you: if I call a supplier and hit an answering machine, they won't be getting a second call.

Next

It comes down to this. If you can't get the basics right in your own business and have foundations of blancmange, you are hardly instilling confidence to me or indeed anyone else who stumbles across your BT Call Minder.

You don't want to make it any harder on yourself by losing enquiries.

So, if you can accept it's going to be tough, there are six key personality traits you are going to need to get you through periods of doubt: self-confidence; tenacity; commitment; judgment; the ability to self-start; and the desire to make a difference.

Self-confidence

Unwavering belief in yourself and in your vision. No one is perfect, so invariably from time to time this will take a knock. Which leads us onto...

Tenacity

The ability to keep your head when everything and everybody around you is falling to bits and others are screaming at you to do other things. You've had a bad few rounds, but remember: you are just one punch away from winning this round.

Commitment

To your business, peers, family, friends, yourself. Never go back, keep moving forward.

Judgment

Your ability to make the correct calls, on business, on people. As long as you can live with the outcome, make that call today. OK, tomorrow. But make that call.

Self-starting

You can only sit around in your underpants for so long before you run out of money, ideas, enthusiasm and excuses. That's what this book is about. Getting off your arse and staying off it.

Making a difference

This could be to your life, family, children, clients, wealth.

Wherever you want to focus, make a difference. The 'making a difference' will glue all the traits above together, all of which are required to be successful.

If you don't possess all of the above, what does that mean? I think it means you need to go and find someone who can plug those gaps in your arsenal or help you develop those traits.

This may be a nutty, bizarre thing, but for some reason when moments of doubt start creeping in, I tune into YouTube and listen to Yazz's *The Only Way Is Up*.

For some strange reason, that song tops up my confidence; remember when I said previously "do something, anything"? It's one of those ritual things, which allows me to shake off negative and unhelpful thought patterns.

Go on! Give it a go right now. Yes, I know you think I've lost the plot, but just try it for me. I'm looking out for you with this book. I have a good finger on the pulse.

Bookmark our Yazz and the Plastic Population and when you are stuck for answers, give it a few listens. It works. Well it does for me.

Here's one thing that I've never heard any business guru talk about. Luck. You can work your socks off 18 hours a day. No such thing as pure luck, so just keep doing the right things, both in life and in business, and the luck will come.

I'm not a golfing man; I've never even picked up a *bat*. Unless of course you count Crazy Golf and I think it's fair to say the holidaymakers at Pontin's in Burnham-on-Sea had rarely before, if ever, witnessed the 'demented windmill' approach until Burton obliged them with a demo.

You've probably heard this before, but golfing legend Gary Player said,

"The harder I practise, the luckier I get."

This same rule applies to you, your life, and your business.

Being 'out there' doing things to the best of your ability, lucky things will happen and leads will come your way. Joint ventures will present themselves, new contacts will be found.

Let's wrap that up neatly in the word 'luck'.

You embarked on a path of self-employment and if things were so great back on the old PAYE, why did you decide to leave in the first place?

I could never work for someone again. I'm unemployable now – in that no-man's land where I've had no option other than to push on. Are you in that same boat?

Think of it like swimming the Channel. You get halfway across and feel you can't go on. It's too painful, so you consider going back to shore.

Hang about, you are halfway across. So you just need to go forward. If you go back to what you know then the chances are you'll stay there.

Yes, I know it's tough at times. *But you can do it.* Remember, I also nearly called it a day on numerous occasions. Nearly.

My mum told me, "The stormier the passage, the more welcome the port". So true.

Although you and I are on different paths, your chosen path and mine are more parallel than you know. That's how it is. Learning is part of the journey. As long you learn from mistakes, then making mistakes is not only forgivable, but essential.

Work when you can, rest when you can, and if "it's too much like hard work" or you are "dreading Monday", you are in the wrong business/job. Find a career you enjoy and you'll never work another day in your life.

If you keep doing what you've always done, don't be surprised when you get the results you've always had. If things aren't going your way, then shake something up by moving things forward; fresh opportunities will surface.

You can only play with the cards you've been dealt.

There will always be situations where you could do with more money and the opportunity to earn it may, or may not, be dealt into your hand.

My journey started off with 'bleat and two veg', remember?

Every step is a lesson learned. Life is a series of branching paths. You reach a fork in the road — go left or go right. Make a call. Choose a path and carry on your journey. You can't ever go back and take the other path and nor should you want to.

4Consultancy > 4Networking.biz > 4Group.net > Brad-Burton.Biz > SpeakerSeeker.net > This book.

All of the above is the result of me telling my employer to shove it up his arse!

Don't be scared to make a decision. I see so many people with a mindset of "any decision is the wrong one". A trait of many a bank manager. By not making a decision you are encouraging a default of leaving things in the lap of the gods. I don't want to be looking to the heavens to be managing my future, do you?

There does come a point when you can go and find a different jockey with a bigger whip, but you're still flogging a dead horse. Coming to terms with a dead idea or a failed dream can be tough, but it is the dreams of the future that matter, not the ones in your past.

I always pick the underdog in boxing and always get it

wrong, I just can't help myself. This is also the case in business life, maybe because I too have been the underdog on so many occasions and wish I'd had a 'Brad' looking out for me.

On a daily basis, I randomly call up 4Networkers, just to get a feel for how things are going. One such time of ringing, I got through to a person and asked how things were going. Normally the response would have been "Fine", but it went something like this.

"Do you want the truth or the BS?"

"Give me the bull."

"Yeah, business is great; I got orders coming from all angles."

"The reality?"

"Debtors piling up, no leads, feeling ill and I don't know where to turn."

"Give me 15 minutes..." I put the phone down and made some calls.

Ringing back, I was able to offer some assistance, advice and contacts; I'd even found a piece of work for him.

The seesaw had tipped the other way within minutes. Things had changed from that person feeling low and tired to elated, upbeat and positive. A whole lot more prepared and up for one more round.

Why? Because he was honest with me. Had he "I'm fine"'d me, I couldn't have helped.

You will have things that are worrying you in your life that can be turned instantaneously from negative to positive by doing something different.

Who around you may be able to help? Collective warmth from

the huddle of the tribe: your friends, your family, your network.

I think it may have been social media expert Seth Godin who said "We are smarter than me."

Wise words from one so bald.

I do a hell of a lot of driving each week, sometimes up to 1200 miles. This affords me a lot of time to make calls and equally to use that time to do some thinking. I got thinking about who I am and why.

I must have been about seven years old, at Saint Boniface's in Salford, Manchester, when I was handed a note written in pencil. It read:

"*Spiderman* is going to **get you**"

I'll always remember; in the bottom right corner was a drawing of a web, complete with a spider hanging down.

Now if the *Spiderman* in this case had been the Stan Lee creation, the webslinger himself, that would have been pretty cool. As an under-ten-year-old imagine the look on my friends' faces as I whizzed around the cobbled streets of Salford, showing my mates the Wall Crawler.

But sadly that wasn't the case. It wasn't *The Amazing Spiderman*, but *Spiderman, The School Bully*. But I'd done nothing wrong!

Have you ever found yourself in life, in the middle of crossfire, when you've done nothing, but for some reason find yourself right in the doo doo?

This was one of those days...

As soon as the school bell rang at 3:30, driven by fear, I

bombed out of the school gates.

"Fight! Fight! Fight!" chanted the kids in pursuit. It's a whole lot more fun chanting than being the fat kid at the front…

I ran and ran down the hill onto the cricket ground until I could run no more. Collapsing, I then got a good pasting from *Spiderman* whilst a gaggle of kids watched.

Wonderfully positive story to end this chapter on, I think you'll agree.

But the moral of this story is this: The longer you run, the weaker you become.

Think about that once more…

The longer YOU run, the weaker you become.

Right now, in your personal/business life, there are conversations you are avoiding and decisions you are ducking. These aren't going to get any easier until you do something. By running away there was only one outcome. It was inevitable that if he hadn't got me that day, he'd have got me the next day or the day after that. The worry of the outcome would have been serious enough to paralyse my ability to play with my 48k *Spectrum* or my *Space Lego*.

Mum would have been on to me and said, *"Are you OK, love?"*

I'd have then said *"I'm fine"*, denying the problem, exacerbating it, only letting her in on the secret after the inevitable outcome and damn good thrashing.

Had I stood my ground at the gates of Saint Boniface's back in 1981, there was an outside chance I would have got a lucky punch, or maybe *Spiderman* really didn't want to fight at all when faced with an active combatant and was only tempted into pursuit because I ran. Bit like a greyhound programmed to chase moving furry things!

We all do this in life: carry burdens that as an unwilling recipient we may have been given, carry them unwilling to unload them.

A psychologist told me that things which happen in the first seven years of our lives are what make us the person we are in adulthood.

Take a trip down your childhood, your memory lane, where does it lead you?

I consider myself a lover not a fighter, probably as I dread to ruin my boyish good looks rolling around on the floor. Besides, my bookings as a *Mr Potatohead* lookalike may dry up.

However, when faced with a difficult situation, I stand and fight every single time. No one gets me over a barrel! Fortunately, due to the superb team that surrounds me, generally speaking, we manage to avoid conflict through negotiation. If 'the hawk' needs to come out, it needs to come out, only to be returned when the threat is removed.

Now we've 200+ linked breakfast groups across the UK and over 20,000 members, we no longer get bullied. Collective strength: the 4N tribe is powerful stuff indeed.

Stop putting off dealing with difficult situations. Deal with them, you'll feel better.

Make decisions quickly and enjoy life more. Sometimes you have to make a decision to know if it's an effective one.

There are no shortcuts, so go ahead and choose a path.

CHAPTER 9

Technology is making the world smaller and I'm getting older and wiser

I often say *"Live the dream"* and for the first time in my life, right now I am. For years I was blowing around, no direction and little focus, with occasional flashes of genius.

It wasn't until the wifey & family came along that it started to come together. Even now I'm not perfect, but I'm getting there. Whilst visiting the North West on business, I drove to the street in Salford, Manchester, where I lived as a kid.

When I arrived, it wasn't the rosy street I once remembered from just under 30 years ago.

Things had changed, now it looked like it should be twinned with the Gaza Strip; engine running, windows up, I'd probably be safer in Gaza.

Thinking about my childhood in Salford got me thinking about my old school chums.

So I went looking on Facebook, searching my hazy memory for the names of people I'd not seen since leaving school back in 1986 and I found some of them!

Friends I haven't seen for 20 years, I've now caught up with in real life; some have done brilliantly, but not everyone has done so well. I've heard stories of births, marriages and of former school pals who are no longer with us.

My Facebook experience has highlighted a couple of things. Technology's making the world smaller and I'm getting older.

How do you utilise this technology and new-found wisdom to make a difference in life and business?

Years ago, and we've all done it, we'd waste office time dicking about on *Solitaire* and *Minesweeper*... now that time is wasted on Facebook and Twitter, the water cooler for the self-employed. However, time is only wasted if it's wasted; right now is the time to embrace this new social media stuff. It works.

Like the hole diggers [spades] before them, social media only works if you use the tools in the right way.

Work or play? That line's being blurred.

In these changing times, we've lost confidence in the banks and the financial markets and MPs are tearing the arse out of expense claims, one spending sixteen thousand quid on cleaning a moat, another two grand on a duck island.

There's a recession of confidence in these former 'pillars of the community'.

So now is a perfect time to get rich in the relationship economy; you have an opportunity to take advantage of this downturn and to build an empire.

An empire built on people and relationships. Think I'm mad?

In the last eight hours I've done 18 'tweets' myself. If you'd like to follow my inane tweeting at *www.twitter.com/BradBurton* you can share the joy of reading "I've just made a nice pot of tea."

Facebook/Twitter — I'm on it, you should be too. Look, this can't just be a tick box exercise, so you've got to be using it because you enjoy it. It's half work/half play and it does work.

In some respects it's the same as posting on *www.4Networking. biz/forum*. This is the place where you'll find me and hundreds of 4Networking members hanging out on a daily basis, asking for help, looking for leads, swapping stupid (and sometimes even funny) gags.

But there is also a sense of belonging, the very thing that you can miss by working in isolation or working away from home.

Remember the boxroom syndrome? Well, social networking can stave that off; when the dark clouds of depression come looking for your friends, you can be there for them as they can for you.

You can't have too many friends, unless of course you're on Facebook.

We are social animals and social networking helps us, but you can't just add a profile and not get involved. It's akin to going fishing, throwing a line out, returning a few days later and complaining that you've not caught anything!

It just doesn't work like that.

Simply registering on them all doesn't make them effective for you. Neither does constantly tweeting on Twitter about how great your business is or what a great a service you offer.

UNFOLLOW

You've got to be interesting, give some value.

As I write this I'm on a train to London from the South

West, using an 8.9" netbook, just slightly bigger than this book you're reading. The days of needing to have muscles like the former world's strongest man, Geoff Capes, to lug your laptop about are no more.

Technology rocks

Netbook £200; 'on the go' 3g dongle, £15 per month. Embrace this technology and use it to stay in contact. Communication is the key. I'm away on average three nights each week and every evening I'll be using that same netbook to speak with my family via webcam from the sanctuary of a Premier Inn.

One of the reasons 4N has taken off across the UK is because of that constant contact; the ability to retain connections between clients and potentials online and offline, day in, day out.

I hear of start-up businesses spending £000s on booking adverts, because they know no better. Stop. Look at social networking as free marketing.

It really is free. It's not wasted time; the only thing it really eats into is a little bit of Jeremy Kyle/*Minesweeper* time.

By all means spend: I actively encourage it, but on the right things.

How about spending some of that saved money on you? Go eat at a posh restaurant.

Of course, you could live on Bran Flakes all your life to save money, but no, it's about living for the moment, living for your friends and family.

One day I'll no longer be here, and sorry to break it to you, neither will you. It is worth checking in the mirror; in the unlikely event of having no reflection, my advice is to stay away from sunlight and garlic bread.

So what's it all about? As I am now nearer 40 than 30, I've taken stock: life is a bit like a *Space Invader* game. Even with the three lives, experience suggests that no matter how well we play, we are going to get hit and we'll all see a 'GAME OVER' one day, so the only thing that is important is how you played and your highest score.

Did you take risks or play it safe?

However you choose to live your life, live it well and be the best person you can be.

I've made some mistakes in my life. Most of them in my early days, aged 21-25, some of them life-changing ones.

But you know what? No one could tell me any different at the time; people tried. But I was unmoved, I knew better. Fortunately, one of those life-changing events fell in my favour; I was literally a foot away from an entirely different future.

Make a difference

Enjoy your life, enjoy your work. If you don't, it's never going to be a real success. Think about it, we've all got just one life. You are wasting it if you're trying to get a high score yet not enjoying the game. It's supposed to be fun!

Don't be anchored by the past, let the present be your future.

Sometimes in life you have to make unavoidable decisions which will cause others pain, but it's like slowly pulling off a plaster.

You are dragging out the pain, so just get it over with by ripping it off as fast as you can. I can talk, I've also done the slow way where you get halfway across and you have to rip it off anyway. So save yourself pain and rip off the metaphorical plaster in your life.

You can have a spoonful of sugar with your medicine, but you've still got to take your medicine.

Here's the older and wiser business bit coming in.

I just spoke at an awesome networking event: 90+ people

in attendance, really well run. Trust me from experience; events like that always have the potential to be flat as a pancake.

A 40-minute seminar based around the stuff in this book. Everyone really enjoyed it, high energy 'edutainment'. You can always tell how successful a speaking gig has been by the feedback and approaches afterwards. The positive response was generally amazing.

However, there was one table of ten who had it in for me. Talking throughout, rolling their eyes at my comments. The amount of negativity from one table was disproportionate.

Fortunately I'm a big, thick skinned Northerner...careful where you put that comma.

Judging by the feedback from the other attendees, they could see what was going on, so it was Table One-Tenth that looked foolish at the end of that day, and in front of peers.

You too are always going to get one table that has it in for you for one reason or another. No amount of trying to win everyone over is going to change that.

Look at Obama – generally regarded as the greatest political leader in a generation. But still there is always someone who wants to have a pop, someone who looks for faults.

You can't please all the people all of the time, so don't even bother. Don't get upset and take it personally.

Equally, if you were one of the people on that table on the evening I'm talking about, ask yourself a question: was this your fight? No, I thought not. Someone roped you into a battle that had nothing to do with you.

Be careful which table you sit on at events, but also in life, because some people will always have their own interests, not yours, at heart.

Whingers & winners

I know who I'd rather surround myself with.

Even to this day we do judge books by their cover.

Look at the cover of this book,

"Voted best business book of 2009*"

*By my mum.

Up until this point, had you even seen the subscript? It may be the reason you picked up the book, having laughed at the gag, or you may have missed it completely and just read "Voted best business book of 2009".

Cheeky. Guerrilla. Effective.

Factually correct? Oh yes, my mum's my biggest fan.

Win some, lose none; cheeky, guerrilla and effective marketing tricks as above can't fail.

That's what marketing is. The things you do to make something easier to sell.

This is that wisdom coming in: look how close you can sail to the wind, without bringing the world down on your head. I'm thick-skinned, so complaints don't really faze me.

Can I be brutally honest? Or continue to be so. When I started 4Networking, I used spam to get me into orbit. I had no budget, no resources; all I had was a great idea and the free time to produce prospective customer lists by looking online for businesses in the local area.

It wasn't spam. It was *smart* spam, aimed squarely at those businesses that would benefit from 4N, and it worked. Three years on, some of those initial recipients of my 'marketing' are still members.

You may be thinking, *"You can't say that!"*

Wrong. I just did; remember, this book is about honesty and sharing with you what worked for me and what didn't.

The way I saw it, if there was no danger of being arrested or having an SO19 armed response unit kicking my front door down, I'd give it a go.

The risks as I saw it:

1.   Get domain blacklisted – use third party email software based in the US.
2.   Have complaints from rival organisations – remove them from my list.
3.   Lose credibility as a businessman – I had none at that time, so nothing to lose.

If you can live with the downside of any decision, go for it. This made complete sense in my own case: the potential benefits far outweighed the possible negatives.

Predictably, I did have the odd complaint, mostly from members of other networks, but sometimes in business,

it's easier to ask for forgiveness than permission.

Nearly four years on, I stand by that decision.

Ironically, if someone were to do the same in 4N land they would get banned from the network. On most occasions it's ineffective because it isn't *smart*, but if positioned correctly it can be damn effective.

Some called it spam; I called it guerrilla marketing and there's a whole load of marketing stuff you can do for £0. Be smart with any low budget marketing.

Use this new technology wisely, it can make or break you.

I talked at the start of this chapter about my childhood; and in doing so I recall that religion didn't sit with me as a kid.

I was the only kid in our school that refused to be confirmed. I put some tough questions to the priest and he didn't give me convincing enough answers. Net result, I was unwilling to go ahead, the only child in the history of our school.

Even back then, as a thirteen year old boy, that was some feat of standing by principle.

For some, religion just creates a whole lot of wars. Granted, for many others it creates a whole lot of hope.

As I near 40, I asked myself, what are my values, what is my code?

My religion?

Braddism was born.

Help many. Hurt few.

Live your life.

If we all lived to those seven words the world would be a better place for you and me.

/Cue rolling hills and children from all around the globe coming together while Michael Jackson's WE ARE THE WORLD plays.

If you are interested in following a life of Braddism, unlike David Koresh, I think the arms we pick up should be not pipe bombs and hunting rifles, but positivity and love. In danger of sounding all kaftans, joss sticks and seaweed sandals, what's really important to you in your life?

Friends, family & health have to be right up there. If you've got at least one of those three, you've a reason to be cheerful.

When the chips are down, look to your family and friends for answers. When I say "look", I mean observe them. The joy children bring playing in a park; the smile of a mum when you pop round with a bunch of flowers; the advice of a father; a friend whose support makes you feel invincible.

Look, like me, you may not have the bright red shiny new Ferrari of your dreams parked outside.

So what?

Ask yourself this question: Why are you doing it? Working long hours, enduring loads of stress and pressure running your business. Is it for that brand new 2010 red Ferrari?

At speaking seminars I often ask the business people in the room whose red Ferrari it is in the car park. Everyone looks around the room. I then ask them who **would like to swap their friends, family or health for a brand new Ferrari.** No hands go up, well occasionally ironically; I then keep upping the offer, adding a million pound pad, five grand cash each week, still no hands **ever** go up.

Trying desperately to avoid sounding like a Yank motivational speaker, you already have at least one thing better than Italy's automotive finest...

Your friends, your family and, all being well, your health.

I'll bet like those in my seminars, you wouldn't swap any one of them for the car/house of your dreams.

So next time you are sat in the office at 11pm, ask yourself this question: what are you doing this for?

Is it for the sports car, or like me when I answered my same question, I found the very thing I was really doing it for was waiting right back at home for me.

That's why you are doing it: for your friends, family and your future, so look after that health!

CHAPTER 10

People buy from people before they buy products or services

U nless the buyer likes the seller, the thing isn't going anywhere. That stands whether you are selling a product, a
service, or just yourself.

OK, when buying plane tickets online, or petrol from your
local station, it's a completely different ballgame. Your decision
to buy wouldn't be based on your relationship with the person
behind the counter, but most probably based on convenience
or price. After all, we've all driven miles out of our way chasing
down the 3p cheaper litre. What's that about?

But in our SME world, if I asked the question:

"Would you do business with people you don't like, know or trust?", most people would say "No".

And that's exactly the question I asked someone recently, who had told me they had been in 4Networking for six weeks and was disappointed that they had received no business.

"Who in 4Networking do you know who likes, knows and trusts you?"

"Fair point," he said.

It's a seesaw. You want business fast and in your impatience feel that others should forgo the usual 'know, like and trust' checks, just for you.

You said so yourself. It doesn't work like that. So you need to work on 'Meet – Like – Know – Trust'. That aside, you also still need to have a decent product.

Then BINGO! I worked it out. Here is the key to selling in networking. I have evolved the MLKT thing from Chapter 4. So how's about this for an equation? We'll call it the Brad Bingo Equation or BB Equation for short.

MLKT + PRODUCT + PRICE + REQUIREMENT = SALE

Also, time goes into this equation. Some people need time to think about buying or need to consult other people. Sellers often try to rush selling, when the other person might well buy, given time to reflect and absorb information. So often, when buyers say "no", the seller thinks they have been rejected out of hand, yet all the buyer needed was more time!

Another reason why networking works – because the buyer to whom you have given more time isn't going anywhere! They can be put on the metaphorical back burner until they are ready to buy or their situation changes.

So many sales are blown by rushing them!

If sales people would get this, they wouldn't feel so rejected when they are turned down. Nor would they assume that the person will never buy and fail to stay in contact with them!

/points at side of head…

Genius

I surprise myself at times, this equation works on so many different levels.

Some people are selling quite complicated products or services and they try explaining it all in 40 seconds along with how clever they are. This doesn't work, because no one else gets it: if other people don't get it, then, again, it's going nowhere.

How do you get round this problem? Start simple, with easy to understand, definable low-risk, value-added offerings – a 'no-brainer sale', so that you start a *billing relationship*.

Once you've established the BB Equation at level one, with a low risk sale, you build the trust to move up to the next level, because you have the contact time to explain the further benefits. This time is combined with the trust built up from the first sale and so the process continues until that customer has built enough trust to recommend and introduce you to others.

But, as I explained, it's not just about selling to the room, it's also about selling *through the room* and this where the 40 seconds becomes even more important – enter the game of the 'Something Sensible Transfer'.

Most people are more focused on their own internal chatter than on what you might have to say, so trying to educate an audience about how good your product is so that they can explain it in turn to other people for you, is quite frankly a waste of time. It's not going to happen.

Everyone is too worried about their own business and how to sell that, to be burdened with trying to sell yours at the same time. To make it worse, they feel scared about explaining the benefits of your product because they don't really understand it themselves. This means they would be doubly scared to answer any question about how your product might stack up against the competition. It's a bit like saying, "I've heard about this really good stuff from some guy I met at a networking event. You should check it out."

It's a great way to lose your reputation. So, back to the 'Something Sensible Transfer'. You need to let the room have a simple-to-understand and memorable 'Something Sensible' **(SS)** that they can take to a target audience **(TA)** because there's something in it for them: a result **(R)**. Then there's a low risk next step to get started on the BB Equation. It looks like this:

SOMETHING SENSIBLE (SS) + TARGET AUDIENCE (TA) + RESULT (R) = NEXT STEP

An example of this in action: a 4Networking member, who has built up an amazing reputation and trust with me, is Liz Cornelius, MD of Somerset-based cosmetic company Unreal *www.unreal.me.uk*. She talked to me about her range of spray-tanning products, part of which features AST, Advanced Seasonal Technology, which is the only solution in the world to include a formulation that means better skin hydration for the different seasons **(SS)**. Nice hook in a competitive marketplace.

Two weeks later, whilst speaking at a networking event in Essex, I got chatting to a lady **(TA)** who runs a chain of beauty parlours. This meant I could instantly share with her my **(SS)**, even with just limited knowledge of Liz's products. The clincher was AST.

Just that one small feature. She wanted to know more. Wallop! Ringing Liz up there and then, I connected them **(R)**. I've since found out that the product is now stocked in all eleven beauty parlours. Over a year this is probably worth £20,000+.

If I hadn't had a **(SS)** hook, there would have been no connection, no £20,000.

How amazing is that? It works.

Two equations in one chapter, I'm feeling all guru-like right now.

Christ, I came over all cufflinky then.

/Sits on naughty step

At another event, someone shared with me how they'd been going to the local Chamber of Commerce for over a year and didn't see much point in going any longer because he knew everyone there and they all knew him.

Later on in the conversation he went on to say that he was beginning to get business and recommendations from these people.

He hadn't noticed the direct link.

I explained to him that the reason he was beginning to get the work was precisely because he'd put in the groundwork and had got to know everyone, and that it was important that he continued going, otherwise he'd just be starting all over again.

Your business environment is constantly changing and just because you think you know someone doesn't mean the job is complete and that you can now pull back.

Think of it like cruising at 70mph on the motorway. Hurrah! I've reached optimum speed: I no longer need to keep my foot on the accelerator. It wouldn't be too long until others overtook you.

If your competitors have more contact with your clients than you, that's how you lose clients. Maintain constant contact: emails, Twitter, networking, lunch, calls, however you do it.

You just have to do it!

It's a general problem with marketing and indeed networking: "50% of it works but I don't know which 50%." There is a time-lag in client response, so you need to stick things out for long enough to see whether they work or not. It's back to the 'swimming the Channel' gig again.

OK! Let's bring it back to you and your business. You may want to grab some paper and scribble down the last three sales you won, along with the last three you lost, and check the components of the BB Equations against the list below:

MLKT – You didn't invest the time in order to build trust.

PRODUCT – Something wrong with the product.

PRICE – Too expensive for the purchaser, you've not sold in the benefits enough.

REQUIREMENT – Do they actually have a requirement for your product or service?

Does it add up? If so, where did you lose those three sales?

If the same thing comes up repeatedly, then it may be worth investigating that area to see if you can plug the gap and ensure future sales.

Product? Price? Requirement?

I just ran that exercise with five of my contacts to test its validity and all of them agreed it works.

Remember the way to go rapidly through the stages of

MLKT and the secret we've established. Be yourself.

In networking terms, consider this: generally speaking, during the 40/60 second round, no one is listening consistently, due to thoughts such as:

"What I should have to eat tonight?"

"I wonder who will be evicted from the Big Brother house at the weekend?"

"Oh my God, it's going to be me very soon! What am I going to say this time? That guy just said what I was going to say."

"I wish I could be more flamboyant, more like that other bloke just now…"

Sorry to break it to you, but it's true.

The elevator pitch bit is all about winning interest with the first sentence. It's a talent-spotting contest that's not selling your products, but selling you.

Because no one is listening anyway.

Give confidence to your audience in you as a person. The product bit follows.

Traditionally, there has been a whole industry set up to try to explain how to develop systems, strategies and disciplines to get other people to help you grow your business. This has led to copious books, workshops, rules, regulations, musts and shoulds, wrapped up as if it was a genuine proven science that should be taken as gospel truth.

The truth of the matter is that you can forget the specialist language, rules and regulations. You just need to understand the basics of business and of human nature.

First of all, you have to learn to row your own boat. That means you need to be able to get your own product or service to market and be able to satisfy your customers – no one else can really do that for you. No one else, except maybe close friends and family, is going to want to support or help you when you are not capable of supporting yourself.

We are talking *inter*dependence here, not setting up a cap-in-hand dependency culture.

For this to work, your business needs strong relationships. How do you build strong relationships? For a kick-off, if I told you how best to go dating according to someone else's rulebook you'd tell me I'm mad. Yet because I tell people not to court their business relationships according to someone else's rulebook, people still say I'm mad.

Another myth is that your business needs referrals to survive. My view is that a business needs *great relationships* to survive.

Hey! I'm not for a minute saying "Don't look for referrals". But over-reliance on third parties is a mistake.

No doubt, referrals rock, of course they do.

However, resting the success of your business and end-of-month mortgage payments on third parties alone is lunacy.

The way I see it, a referral culture is akin to that of a drug or alcohol dependency culture. Your business needs to stand on its own two feet and, just like drinking, it's OK in moderation and as long as you don't come to depend on it to function.

No one who has ever asked me for a referral has ever had one given. I pass on leads because it's the right thing to do, based on the best person for the job. I don't need to be prompted or asked and I suggest that those same rules apply to you.

Last week alone, 27 leads or connections were made. No ceremony behind the passing of those leads and in each instance it was just as a result of being the right fit.

The era of the referral fairies has passed: it's now just a good old relationship economy.

The world has changed, the business world has moved on. Have you?

The nonsense that was perpetuated in one book I read, about how you should respond when you receive a business card: apparently, you should "covet it in both hands; stare intently at it (feigning interest) before placing it in your top pocket."

What a crock!

Once you've be given the business card, just put it in whichever pocket you want to. It's not Japanese *meishi* etiquette (the art of card-swapping) that's important, or what pocket you put it in. It's about the follow up.

People buy from people, before they buy products or services.

Metaphor time. Some networks have rules which effectively close the extended business world to them — think of them as like little fish tanks, fifteen or so fish in each of them. Each tank sits alongside others, but you are forbidden (it's considered disloyal) to jump into another tank.

That ends today's Brad metaphor session, or does it? You don't get off that easily.

Following that fish analogy, what we wanted with 4N was to create a big lake teeming with life, with the opportunity go where you want, when you want. Although you may get lost now and again, you'll find new friends and maybe a new home in the process. You stand and fall based on your ability: it's a true meritocracy.

Classic story. A few years back now, in the early days of 4Networking, one of the guys was cowering behind a chair, shaking like a leaf...

"There's another printing bod in the room", he gasped.

"Shit, I only just noticed", I lied.

"Wh-wha-wha-what should I do?"

"Look, I've an idea. He's near the coffee station right now, so I'll go up to him, keep him talking, and then when his back's turned you *run up to him and hit him over the head with a candlestick holder and cave in his skull; we can get rid of the body later."*

"Are you being serious?"

"No, Kev, no I'm not. Go up and talk to him."

Sure enough, he did, and they hit it off beautifully (strictly metaphorically...), rapidly going through the meet, like, know and trust gears. Just over a month later, their relationship bloomed, with even visits to the golf course: competitors had morphed into friends.

Mix business with pleasure, why not? There are thousands of examples of it working and of course, there will always be the odd horror story of it all going wrong. Never play to fail.

The love affair didn't end there.

When a £30,000 job came up, the printer at the centre of the *Candlestick Assassination Plot* didn't have the capacity that Kev had and, where normally he would have turned down a job of that size, this time around the shared resource, collaboration and completion meant they could win, fulfil and split the profits from a sizeable piece of work.

Hurrah!

Hang about? People in the same 'business category', doing real and significant business together. Why? Because people buy people, before they buy products and services.

It was a shock to Kev's system. For years in his previous networking life, he'd been conditioned through 'training' to think that competition was BAD and that hiding behind a wall with his networking gang, lobbing bricks at the competition, isolated from the reality of market forces, meant safety in business. "The stabilisers need to come off the bike one day," I told him.

The idea that you should be fighting constantly with your 'competition' is outdated, naive and unproductive for your business. Embrace your competition.

Since that day, I've clocked up loads of examples of collaborations. You've been sold a porkie, stop perpetuating it and recognise that business has moved on since the 80s.

Remember when I asked, would you go to a trade show if your competitors were there? Would you go to a networking event if your competitors were there? What's the difference?

The internet means that the Chinese walls in business that once existed have been torn down so that there is no hiding place from alternative prices and quotes.

The best way you can win the hearts, minds and continued business of your target audience is through damn good service, prices and innovation. Protectionist business practices are no longer winning.

Cash inducement fees for passing leads. I'm not sure about this, do they work for you? For me, I would never swap out an existing established relationship just for a monetary inducement.

Go after, or create, opinion formers. These are people who are connected to lots of other people or are in the know about what you do and have experienced it. The way to do this is to give amazing value, including giving stuff away for free. You know what? I do 1-1 coaching with a difference: I work with businesses for two hours, blah blah blah, but when I first started out on this gig, I gave away loads of sessions to 'opinion formers' for free.

Know what? It worked. I now get approached on a weekly basis by someone that has heard about my GOYA programme, as a result of my opinion formers. Create yourself a *conversational strategy* and get people talking about you or your business.

Due diligence is being done on you all the time, even when you're not there.

It's no secret that at 4NHQ we use a third party telephone answering service, *www.kbswindon.co.uk*. We've been with this Swindon-based company since late 2005. Starting out on a £35 monthly retainer, the fee has grown as the network has grown; it's now in excess of £1k per month.

We only pay when our members use it, so it's wonderfully scalable.

During a 1-1 at a networking meeting, I chatted with a new member who runs a similar answering service business. In the conversation, she told me that, as we're 4Networking, if I swapped the business over to her, she would give me a discount of 50%, saving me thousands per year. She thought she had it sussed.

She could have offered it to me for free, as my answer would have been the same.

"Not interested"

Yup, we could save £5k+ a year, but my trust and credibility across the UK would be shot to pieces. The damage to my reputation by being Mr Mercenary would far outweigh the projected savings. It also would mean that the next person who came along with a special offer could take the business.

Where's the loyalty?

Businesses need to make money in order to provide awesome service. That's what it's all about.

Awesome service. Get that right and you don't need to ask for the referral because everyone talks about it.

I threw a quote back recently for being too cheap, as in "please make it more". It's about value. I've grown to respect it, but am I mad as a badger? No. I did this because I value people and I value both my customers and my suppliers.

Have a nosey at an email I received: it's another real example of how things in business may well be changing for the better.

From: Robin Parker [mailto: robin@ccprinting.co.uk]
Sent: Thu 30/07/2009 11:06 AM
To: Brad Burton
Subject: 4Community Mag - CCP [Scanned]

Brad
Number of pages of magazine has increased (4pp cover and 48pp text Total 52pp) but managed to keep the cost the same as previously quoted. Thought that might make you happy!
Regards
Robin

I am blown away by this. Robin could have charged me a few hundred quid more. I wouldn't have batted an eyelid. But he didn't.

Why would he do that? He never cc'd anyone in on the email or to my knowledge told anyone about this: he did it because he values our ongoing business relationship and maybe because he also recognises me as an opinion former.

True to form, I thought I'd share it with the readers of this book as an absolutely amazing example and a lesson of how to generate more business during the 'slow down' by actively retaining and valuing your existing clients.

Robin Parker, *www.ccprinting.co.uk*, you are a fine example to all of us.

Look after existing clients as much as you do new ones. Deepen your network before you widen it. Scurrying around hoovering up more business cards that you don't follow up is a waste of good deepening effort. In the past I've been guilty of it myself. So now I practise what I preach.

Do this, regardless of how funky your website is or how shiny your brochures are.

And remember, unless the buyer likes the seller, it isn't going anywhere.

CHAPTER 11
I don't do Chapter 11

The Yanks do, when their businesses are in trouble; why copy them??

You *really* don't want another cut-out picture of me, surely.
Make some useful notes instead.

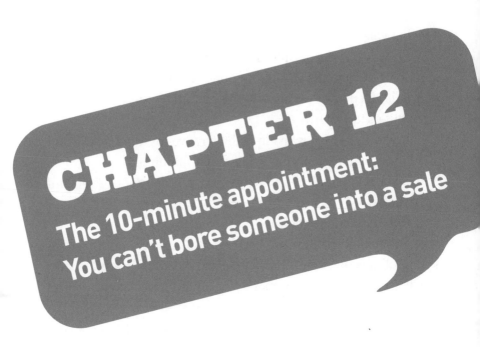

CHAPTER 12

The 10-minute appointment: You can't bore someone into a sale

In my early days of self-employment, I would spend weeks trying to get an appointment to see a potential client. The routine would be: send them a letter, give them a call and sometimes even I got lucky.

Most times I didn't, but I still had to go through the ritual: Throw+mud+walls=success.

So what's the alternative?

In business, you need appointments; if you're not sitting in front of people, nothing happens. Unless of course, you're *Amazon.com*.

The success, or more generally, failure, of my efforts was decided by so many factors. Was the mailer itself any good? Did the right person open it? Did it get opened at all? Did they actually need what I was selling? Was the follow-up call any good?

The list was endless.

So many variables and uncertainties in the process; and at any point during this strung-out, long-winded, labouring caper, you only needed to put one wrong foot along the way and you were out of the race.

If you fail, the downside is that you've invested weeks and shed loads of energy trying to get that appointment.

Let's take stock here: we're just talking about *"get that appointment."*

Appointment – not sale.

You had no option. You had to do this carpet-bombing marketing alongside some smart targeting. All sounds a bit poncy, but it was all part of the marketing mix – don't forget; I'm an award-winning marketer.

So, along came this networking lark, which has created a framework for meeting people, with some networks and meetings being more effective than others. We'll come back to networking later.

Back to the conventional approach to getting appointments.

Now, let's say that you managed to get through to the decision maker and speak to him or her. In my experience, the appointment date was always a mythical 'six weeks into the future' and as the day neared, something always seemed to come up, pushing it back even further.

I'd like to share with you a story from my life before self-employment.

I worked at a security firm with high, high-end stuff and I headed up the company's marketing. I used some corking tricks in order to get to see the European Security Director for a household-name bank based at Canary Wharf.

He had an eight digit budget for security. The one above £100 million: £1 billion or something. Big money anyway. How did I know that? He said so whilst speaking at some 'cufflink' security conference or other I attended.

Judging by what he said at the seminar, it was clear he and I had so much in common. Like me, he loved the sound of his own voice. Following on from the conference I sent him a letter, stating how much I enjoyed his (boring) speech.

I kept on his case, ringing every day...as in every day for six weeks. Take it from me: it's absolutely essential that you continue to ring prospects until you get a "no". Anyway, back to the story: I was finally transferred through to him. He said, "Sorry I've not come back to you. I'm really interested in what you sent me. I've been meaning to get my manager who deals with the UK to give you a call." So I said, "If you give me his details, I'll give him a call right away."

This whole thing was most likely a brush-off; whether it was or it wasn't, I had to go for it.

So, ringing him, I mentioned his director wanted us to sit down and sure enough, I clinched the appointment.

Geezuz! Look at how much work was involved in getting the contact details of the right bloke!

So there I was, sat in the posh reception of a bank HQ in Canary Wharf, on my best behaviour, waiting to see Mr Smith. I was made to wait in reception for 15 minutes longer than the time of the scheduled meeting. It's all a bit combative, this selling gig. There's a definite "you're the seller, I'm the purchaser, therefore I have the upper hand" thing going on. OK, so that's a generalisation, but there's not a sales person in this land who's not found themselves in that situation.

As the clock ticks, the nerves start building. After all, so much depends on this deal. My sales director at the time had been on my case.

A meeting with a 'top three' bank. Impressive stuff! Massive news! The office was awash with excitement that I'd nailed this appointment.

Actually, the whole situation was a bit surreal – akin to that bit on *The Apprentice* when the receptionist says, "Sir Alan will see you now, you can go through."

My 'target' came out to greet me, apologising for keeping me waiting. I stood up and we shook hands. Within about five seconds, I realised this was going nowhere.

However, we're now in 'business meeting mode', so what comes next?

"How was the drive in?"

"Yeah...A13 wasn't too bad."

Small talk, small talk, small talk etc etc etc

"Can I get you a drink?" All very civil. Sitting in the plush office, we got down to business. 'Business' in this instance was that God-awful three minute wait as you small talk whilst the laptop powers up. Then the sweat on my fingers caused the mouse pad not to work, so I felt like I was playing a corporate version of 'pin the tail on the donkey', trying to get my mouse cursor on the correct .ppt file on the desktop.

Hurrah! The Powerpoint loaded up.

Six minutes into an hour meeting and guess what? It's just NOT WORKING.

He didn't like me – honestly – and I didn't like him: and the worst thing is...we both knew it.

Sooo, looks like I have 54 minutes of bullshit to go. He's not buying. It's worse than that. He's not interested in the slightest.

So what should I do? I know! Bundle more statistics into the pitch. Don't panic, Brad, you've got another 27 Powerpoint slides, so we can both hide from the reality of the situation.

I was wasting my time and his – and yet that's how it played out. 35 minutes into the hour meeting and it's about the right time to call it a day.

"Really interesting (boring) presentation, Brad. I'll get back to you if we can free up the budget", which translated into "I've no interest in your product: I only took the appointment because you cleverly managed to sort it with my director."

On top of the wasted meeting time, I'd spent hours prepping, hours ringing, two hours travelling, to be rewarded with, to all intents and purposes, a "not interested".

You've either presented, or been presented to, in a meeting like that, at some point in your life. We all have. A massive waste of energy. Having said that, six years on, it's made a rather poignant story in this book, so things happen for a reason. Hopefully you can avoid the same mistake.

So, what's the solution? I reckon we have it sussed. As you learned earlier, in 4N land, at our networking meetings we have 3 x 10-minute one-to-one appointments within group time, with people you want to meet or who want to meet with you. You base your choice of people to meet on what they say or how they handle themselves during the 40-second 'talent spotting' session round the table.

Tim Johnson said, "Let's call the 1-1 rounds, 'appointments'."

I said,

"Don't talk daft. You can't call 10 minutes an appointment."

At the time I thought he was insane, bonkers, and dismissed it with a Darth Vaderesque wave of the hand.

Driving from HQ to home that evening, my old school mentality kicked in. I thought, "10 minutes isn't long enough; I need an hour for my sales appointments." My internal voice then said, "Sorry to break it to you, but these are not sales appointments."

10 minutes is most definitely an appointment, it's long enough to establish whether or not you like the person enough to move things on.

Back to the real hard work world of winning real world business appointments.

To get an appointment you need to get past 'the gatekeeper'.

Their job, like that of a bank's computer, is to say "No", regardless of how sensible your product is or how perfect a fit. Their job is to brush you off.

Old school, out-dated thinking. Me? I just love to receive sales calls, as long as they are sensible, smart and relevant. Bring 'em on!

Back to the professional head-shakers. They're called PAs.

"Hi! Is that Mr Jones' PA? Yes, it's Brad Burton from the Royal Mint. I've £1,000,000 in cash in reception and all I want for it is a quick meeting with him and it's his..."

"I'm afraid Mr Jones isn't available right now."

"Any idea when he'll be back?"

"Can I ask with what it's in connection?"

"Yes, as I said a second ago, I'm from the Royal Mint and I really have got £1,000,000 in cash in reception and all I want is a quick five minute chat and he can have it."

"Is he expecting your call?"

And so it goes on. Totally nuts.

Now if, like my bank story, you somehow manage to Jedi mind-trick the PA, or in my case, the 'European Security Director', what's the point? Look at my story: massive investment on all fronts, just to get blown out. Why? Because I never got buy-in from the person I ended up meeting.

The thing is fraught with problems. It can fall over at any step along the way. It's totally nuts and an inefficient use of time in doing business, sorry, getting appointments. But do it you must, 'cos there is *no* alternative. Or is there?

There are all manner of tricks and strokes you can pull to get an appointment. I'll share some with you in the next paragraph. However, if you do get a result, you are still eons away from it magicking into an invoice.

There are some tried and tested tricks I've used to get in front of people. These work!

Print a letter upside down on your letterhead and send it out. Guaranteed to get a response when you speak to people. They say, "Did you realise you'd printed it upside down?"

Look for prospect businesses within one square mile of where you live.

I'm not gonna get all Greenpeace on you about cutting emissions through less travel, because this is all about contacting businesses within that target area. "As a 'neighbour', I thought it would be useful for us to meet, as I'm only down the road in xxx," is another great hook.

Print and then screw up your letter so it's scrunched up into a ball. Send it in an envelope. At the bottom, so it's somehow visible, put "We do XXX (job)...This paper is the only thing we screw up."

Chop a £5 note in half and staple one half to a letter saying,

"I'd like to meet you so that we can both make money."

I sent piping hot pizzas to journalists in London. The pizza box lid had a picture of me smiling, winking, with a pizza box in my hand. Then the words: "There is such a thing as a FREE LUNCH. WWW.BRADBURTON.BIZ" That was it!

A day later, some calls. This worked beautifully, winning me loads of appointments and plenty of 'column inches'.

You have to dance around the handbag for a bit before you invite someone back to your place for coffee.

Print something on the outside of the envelope which gets attention, causes a smirk. Here's an example: "LETTER MAY CONTAIN TRACES OF NUTS."

With letters, handwrite the envelopes. We tried it with 1000 printed and 1000 handwritten. We had four times the level of response from the handwritten version.

So, your letter is about creating impact in order to get that 10 minute appointment. That's it. It's not about selling.

Some people get caught out by this schoolboy selling mistake. It's a bit like a CV: its purpose is to get you the interview, not the job.

In terms of the phones, there are a few strokes you can pull:

Get a PA, OK, not really…but get someone who has a brain and can pretend to be one. Get them to ring up and say:

"Hi, it's Mr XX's PA here, I've Mr XX on the phone and he'd like a director-to-director call with Mr Y please."

That's it. End of.

If pressed, try using an 'exec call'. It means absolutely nothing. Nothing! But saying "exec call" sounds like the other person should know what it is: confused, they often put you through.

"Hello, is that Mr.Bobbit's PA? I have an exec call for him."

The other route is...

Out of all the clever tricks that you can pull off, the most effective one is someone else selling you in. Load them up with 'Something Sensible' about your business and enough collateral and they will sell you in.

Get this: generally, you're still about six weeks away from a meeting with someone you've had little or no contact with.

But I recently placed a £5,000 job with someone whom I'd met for just ten minutes.

So, try angling for ten minutes "when I'm passing". There is something wonderfully disarming about that. It's an approach that works beautifully. I know because I've used it and pulled it off. The whole purpose is just to nip in for a quick coffee, oh, and a quick chat.

Equally, no one likes being 'sold at'. Listen up!

Create the situation where it's not a hard sell, but an easy buy.

Don't sell. Create the conditions where people buy. An example of this which you'll get is the iPod. Have you ever heard of anyone going into Comet and saying, "Excuse me young man, can you tell me the benefits and features of an iPod?"

It just doesn't happen. The purchaser is just that, someone who knows what they want, so it's more a case of:

"Excuse me. Do you have an iPod in stock?"

"Sure, which colour? Red, black or white?"

The sell has been done upfront. No hard sell: an easy buy.

Smart marketers are locking onto this. Marketing is what you do to make things easier to sell.

"Can we do business?" type meetings — 10 minutes is perfect. I'm totally converted and you will be too.

Create the conditions in your appointments where the person sat opposite wants to buy, not necessarily your product/service right now, but wants to buy *some more time with you* so that you can explain more about your offering.

Do a taster gig, low price, free. Build up to proper jobs. Gain their confidence. As MD of several companies, that's exactly how I get hit at all the time within 4N. It's a smart, smart move, to get a low-level billing relationship underway and then build on it.

Someone told me:

"Ten minutes isn't long enough to explain what I do."

Listen, I can explain the Apollo Moon landings in fifteen seconds.

"NASA plans and builds a rocket over a decade; three blokes get in a big rocket in 1969.

It takes off successfully, orbits the Moon, deploys a lunar landing module which lands on the Moon; two of them walk on the Moon. One says, "One small step for man, one giant leap for mankind". They load up with Moon rock and return safely to Earth, hailed as heroes at tickertape parade."

Are you honestly telling me that your business offering is more complicated than the Apollo Moon landings?

No, I didn't think so. Now, after reading that, boil your business down to fifteen seconds, which you know off pat. Not just facts but fill it with some hooks and excitement.

So the key is to get your succinct pitch right; if you can't get it to land in 15 seconds or in ten minutes, then it's unlikely you've got a chance in one hour, or at all.

Create hooks which can be picked up by the other person, something to pique their interest to proceed.

I have just been watching some re-runs of *Dragons' Den* on TV, and found myself making snap judgements from a three minute pitch, about who they are, their competency and so forth.

You really don't need an hour. Unless of course you are sold on the idea in the first few minutes, and want to know more. I guarantee it's a whole lot easier to sell to a busy business person in a ten minute coffee and chat sesh than it is in an hour-long presentation.

Michael Goody of *www.Coloursells.com* shares with me his experiences of the ten minute appointment within 4Networking meetings:

"The point I always try to get across to new members is the ability to make completely new relationships with the most unlikely people. When I first started networking and discovered there was a graphic designer in the room I would go in like an *Exocet* to make an appointment.

I soon realized that this train of thought wasn't as productive as I had anticipated, as the designer already knew a couple of dozen printers — and since I knew the same number of designers, this wasn't the great opportunity I had thought.

Now, going to the other extreme, when I end up at 4N as 'Billy No Mates' and have 1-2-1s with trades or professions with which I have no common ground, I have found that these contacts have been most productive.

They meet a printer who they can recommend and in turn

I can promote their business. Because we both don't know any people in each other's profession, it makes the contact much more valuable."

Back in my old 4Consultancy days, I was a little bit 'cufflinky' to be honest, I knew no better. But I'd use an A4 presenter, wonderfully visual, had loads of hooks in it, so I suggest you do the same: whizz through it if need be, it gives you a safety net if you lose your way during a presentation.

If I asked you to increase your average weekly sales by 50% in a week, how confident would you be? Some would say that it's nigh on impossible, otherwise you'd have sorted it already.

Yes, it'd be a challenge, but there are circumstances in which you could do it and repeat it consistently.

Grab your visualisation cap.

Imagine the same challenge, except there's an additional factor.

A bloke dressed head-to-toe in black, wearing a balaclava, armed with a loaded .45 Heckler & Koch pistol, pressed against your head. **Manchester Motivation.**

"Increase your weekly sales by 50% or for you, there'll be no next week. Understand?"

That increase doesn't seem so unattainable after all now. You would make it happen somehow, it would cease to be a problem. You'd commit to 100% increase in sales for ever more to avoid a bullet in the head. Either you or the problem would cease to be, and the chances are, the problem would be the one to go.

What's changed?

Your motivation! Now I'm not sure kitting sales managers or partners out with small arms is the optimum way to motivate yourself in business, medium to long-term, but my point is made. It's all about motivation. Don't let it get to that stage. Start right now to increase your sales: move your business forward by imagining that you do have a gun pressed to your head and the pressure's on.

Work out how you would do it if your life depended on it and go ahead and make it happen!

Move fast, move on, put fire down-range. Don't chase rainbows. If you've given it your best shot and they don't 'get it', regardless of whether it's your fault or theirs, move on. You can't afford to keep anchored to this.

Hello
10 minutes
No hard sell
Easy buy
Bottom line me
Goodbye

You can't bore someone into a sale: 10 minutes is always long enough.

You can't bore someone into a sale. Write it down.

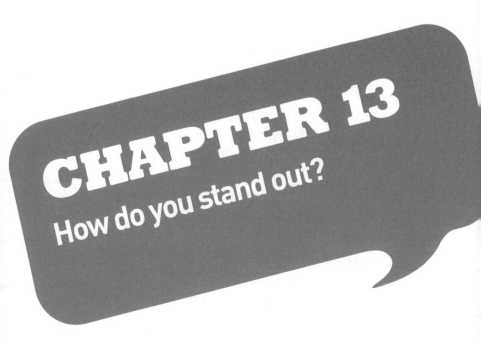

CHAPTER 13
How do you stand out?

When I do any public speaking, it's likely you'll see me with a pizza box in my hand. It's a prop, a gimmick. But it works on so many levels and I'll explain why.

It gets people talking about it, cracking gags and heckling, instead of it just being some bloke stood in front of them doing a seminar. This is now some 'weird bloke with a pizza box', what's that all about? It keeps up interest until the real show starts.

Initially it gave me comfort, a bit like Princess Diana used to carry a bunch of flowers because she didn't know what to do with her hands during public engagements.

It's obviously a throwback to my delivering pizza days and it allows me to interweave that element and the 'supportive wife' into the story. Apologies for the speech marks. I did promise I wouldn't use them again, didn't I?

No doubt some people think "What an idiot"; some get it, some don't. But I guarantee one thing: either positively or negatively, the vast majority will talk about it. Either way I'm happy. It's *free marketing*.

So how do you stand out in your business?

You do stand out, right?

I'm sorry to break it to you, but if you don't, it's going to come down to price every time. Do you really want to win jobs only because you're the cheapest?

The way to stand out in business is by being different and by doing things differently.

4Networking is different and better than any other business network in the UK. Now, I would say that, but it's our decision to be different that makes us better.

Others tried to copy the former market leader and guess what, *lost every time*. 'No names', but the former generally-regarded-number-two in the UK networking scene is now generally-regarded-number-three.

Why?

Because they copied the former market leader.

As in one-hundred-per-cent copied. Try as they might to say "We do this or that differently", I'm sorry: it was a carbon-copy, an imitator, without sufficient differentiation.

Differentiate, or it's down to cheapest price or who has the bigger advert.

An example of someone who does things differently, but damn effectively, is Tom Lawrence from TLC Office Supplies, *www.tlcbusiness-supplies.co.uk*, the only company I know in the UK that gives all its customers <u>free biscuits</u> on orders over £70. Every time our order from TLC arrives in the office, we're all fighting over who opens the box. Let's face facts, it's not for the box of ballpoint pens or 12 pack of Tippex.

Is their Tippex cheaper? Knowing Tom, it probably is, but the truth is I neither know nor care.

Why? Because TLC gives us **FREE** biscuits and *great service*.

See, the free biscuit ruse would not be enough of a sweetener to stay if we received bad service. But it is enough to ensure that the girls at 4NHQ are less inclined to change suppliers, even if the slickest of sales people come knocking at the office.

Do things differently, because it works, people talk to you and people talk about you.

Billy Bear ham

You may see this stuff at deli counters. It's frigging *processed* ham, shaped like a bear's head. It's more expensive than conventional ham per 100grams, yet it probably costs the same to produce. It's not about the ingredients they use; it's all about "doing something to convert it into something different."

But guess what? That's the stuff my five year old boy Ben wants...in fact *needs*. The purchasing decision is not about superior taste, quality or price; on the contrary, it's driven by my boy. Why? Because its niche position is 'funky, different and attractively packaged'...for a five year old.

I'm not sure how impressed dinner guests would be...I may well try that just to be different.

You can learn a lot about marketing by looking at *Billy Bear* ham.

For Chrissakes, it's even called *Billy Bear*: every element makes kids desire it. Genius! Next time you see it at a deli counter, enjoy the smile it creates.

Who are the best sales people in the world? If you have a

young family you'll know the answer.

"Dad, can I have an ice cream?"

"No son, not today."

Tears, tantrums or "I love you dad…"

Hmm

"Did you want one flake or two with that, son?"

Back to creating difference: 50p worth of raw plastic can be moulded either into a £2 cup or a £10 box of Lego.

Lego Group introduced plastic building blocks in 1947, but it wasn't until 1958 that the Lego bricks we all know and love were created. I played with them back in 1981-85, a fine vintage for *Space Lego* I'm sure you'll agree.

Fast forward to 2009 and my boy Ben even has a bucket of the stuff that I played with.

My point?

It took eleven years for them to develop it from initial concept to something resembling modern day Lego.

At any point in those *eleven years*, it could have been canned as a bad idea, not developed, or made 'different'.

Fifty years on, Lego is still growing as a business, developing ever more inventive ways of emptying consumers' pockets, with plastic bricks being joined by theme parks, computer games and merchandising.

The same goes for you and your thoughts. You can create something that fades out or something that changes the world forever.

4Networking will transform business networking for the majority of SMEs in the UK…

Sorry, I mean the world over. It will happen and you can quote me on it.

Being different is a journey that starts with you.

Pizza box in hand, I spoke recently at a CIMA meeting, The Chartered Institute of Management Accountants. The gig was surprisingly well received. Well, you know the stereotype of a dynamic accountant? He stares at your shoes, not his own.

Halfway through I think, "I'll have a laugh here", so I say:

"You know what? I'm actually in the market for a new accountant. Who would like my business?"

After what seemed like nearly an hour, fifty sheepish accountants' hands slowly rose up.

"You sir, in the front row. Why should I choose you?"

"Because we're professional," he blurted out, bold as brass.

"Fantastic," I said. "Are there any other accountants in the room who are professional?"

It was a cheapish trick on my part, but the point was made.

You have to distinguish yourself from the rest of the pack.

It can't just be a mission statement because that means naff all printed on the back of your business card. You have to live it – that's the difference.

If I asked your best client how you are different from your competition, what would they say? What do they like about you? What would they say about you and your approach? Have a think about that for a second.

I pride myself on being full of energy and drive, but also being approachable. Man of the people. I live this and that's what I am. I'm not method acting.

I'm going to move onto 4Networking's differences here. This really isn't a sales pitch, but an insight into how being fundamentally different to any other networking group in the world has paid dividends. Here are some examples:

1. Members are encouraged to attend any of the 200+ groups, right across the UK.
2. An online community plus offline group meetings which run Tuesday-Friday on a fortnightly cycle.
3. 50% social/50% business culture
4. Lightly moderated online community
5. Flat structure, benign dictatorship: anyone who needed to be fed into the wood-chipper had already gone in...
6. Hands-on board level commitment
7. Non-franchised model and continuous heavy re-investment
8. 8-10am meetings: practically the afternoon in break-fast networking terms
9. No compulsion to attend or to bring visitors or to refer business – yet everyone does
10. Three 10-minute 1-2-1 appointments at every meeting

Remember, I was told on Day One: *"It'll never work."*

Our list of distinctive features really does go on and on, so let's go back to that original question, how do you differentiate yourself?

If all you can say about your business is the exact same as the market leader in your locale, then you're never going to be the market leader.

Funnily enough, when we first came up with the concept of 50% social, 50% business, I was labelled "mad as a badger". Bonkers. Doolally. Screw loose...

A 'lightly moderated online community' which does not get involved if members start punching holes out of each other. MAD. Bonkers. Doolally. Screw loose...Nuts.

Everyone loves a pub fight, as long

as they're not the one in it.

Heated forum debates are great for internet traffic and anyway, if you do intervene, all you achieve is a masking of the issues. By allowing a brawl to sort itself out, it means the dispute won't manifest itself elsewhere.

The list of 4N things which have been labelled "mad" is as long as my arm. You will get this all the time when you do things differently in business: it's only when it works that madness gets recognised as genius. But you won't know if you're a genius until you get out there and try something, er, mad.

In just over a year, we've gone from being just within the top 10,000th most visited websites in the UK to a top1000 player.

Mad or genius?

Here's how it goes:

MAD>>>>MAD>>>>MAD>>>>GENIUS

Innovate your products. Innovate your approach. Never stop moving.

There are 'rivals' looking at what we're doing now, intent on copying our model. Let them go for it.

As I mentioned just now, you will never be market leader simply by copying the market leader.

You can copy a format, but unless you've got a nutcase at the helm, with a mix of three eclectic directors, all joined by a central and collective mindset on "making a difference before we make money", then forget it, because there's no money in it. Well, not for the first three years anyway.

When you create something different, someone will be looking to rubbish your ideas or copy your innovation. But a moving target is a whole lot more difficult to hit.

So this "being different" thing isn't just a case of being different for the sake of it.

What are the occupational hazards of networking every day? It's no accident that I'm this fat, have a cholesterol score of 8.7 and should be dead. Remember, someone asked me about my exit strategy. I'm hoping I'll go out on my shield at a breakfast meeting, having been taken out by excessive 'widowmakers'. In Civvy Street these are known as 'hash browns'.

Get yourself a gimmick, a memorable hook. Mine's the pizza box, for obvious reasons (see Chapter 2). If I'd delivered pizzas when I was 17, as a casual job, then it wouldn't be worth telling the story, the box would have no significance. It's the circumstances I was in that have turned the box into a symbol, a motif, summing up everything about how tough it is to transfer from employment to self-employment.

When I first fielded the pizza box, I was so embarrassed, unsure and uneasy about it, but now I'm rarely seen out in networking public without it.

At a trade show in Harrogate, I turned a negative, something I was once ashamed of, into something I'm now proud of. And that's what you need to do. I'm in the loo and overheard a conversation:

"Did you see that nutter with the pizza box? What was that all about?"

"No idea." As I walked past I said "yeah, what a loon."

They remembered the pizza box more than they remembered me. Later on in the day, someone would know who I was because I'd talk to them and it'd all make sense.

In this ever busier business world, you have to make an impact.

IT'S FREE MARKETING!

Here's a bit more on the subject of standing out from the crowd.

I was holding a seminar at Network Central in Somerset, an absolutely massive networking event which had over 1000 networkers attending.

All the other commercial networks were in attendance, so I thought: how could I garner attention? The pizza box just wasn't enough. So I donned a pink cowgirl hat, complete with pigtails, and walked around the show. I could see reactions, from absolute horror to bemusement to laughing out loud. Bottom line, my seminar had standing room only, a complete sell-out.

It worked.

Remember the *Milk Tray Man* advert and calling card? It's just a cheap box of chocolates… but hang on, all of a sudden it's romantic and it encourages fellas to buy *Milk Tray* over other brands. Why? Because ladies buy into romance and blokes buy into the action aspect and so feel quite cool in the process.

Everyone wins.

Blokes are rubbish at buying presents. Well, I am. For my second wedding anniversary I had no idea what to buy my wife. Apparently a £20 Asda gift voucher just doesn't cut it. Anyway, I'd treated Kerry to one of those the previous year, so this time I thought I'd *surprise* her.

Someone told me about a place in Bristol called *Build-A-Bear Workshop*. It's a fully themed shop where, as the name suggests, you build a bear. Choose the type of bear, the colour, the clothes, sunglasses etc and then get to stuff it with some candy floss looking gubbins, using some machine within the shop.

I ended up spending £22 on a stuffed bear, but it was worth it. Why? Because I got to put three little pillow hearts in it, one from each of us in the family. The assistant then made me perform the ritual of kissing each of the hearts, making a wish, spinning around three times, before sealing up *Braddy Bear*.

A rotund and rotating 36-year-old fat Grant Mitchell look-a-like in a crowded shop on a busy Saturday: I'll be honest with you, it wasn't a great look.

I bought much more than a bear that day: I bought into the *Build-A-Bear* experience.

About my wedding...we were married in June 2007. Not one to miss an opportunity, I thought, "Right, Wedding4Networking." If you think I'm joking, Google "wedding4networking": you'll find photos along with a five minute radio interview from 4Networking Taunton on the morning of our wedding.

It's a special day and should be treated as such. It was indeed a special day and it featured something unique: the world's first networking event at a wedding reception: 100+ networkers swapping business cards.

You can't do that.

Why not?

Says who?

One moment in time, but used twice over: for an awesome wedding *and* for a unique networking event. What a talking point, and a damn good party with my networking pals!

Be different: create a talking point as part of your conversational strategy.

Creative house *www.Kimeera.com* staged an *Office Dance Off*.

You've never seen anything like it: all 14 staff coming out from behind a tinsel curtain and dancing, albeit in a tongue-in-cheek (facial, not butt) manner. Naturally, it was filmed and uploaded for all to see on YouTube.

A bean counter accountant may have seen this as folly. One hour x 14 wages for effectively 'dicking about'. 14 man hours isn't cheap. Who cares? Sometimes you have to shove ROIs up arses and just do it. In this case, the dance-off worked as it has generated thousands of views on YouTube. With my marketing hat on, all this far outweighs the initial upfront cost. The morale of the team increased, the number of people who now know about Kimeera has soared. Where's the downside? Are they still 'professional'? Absolutely! Look at their work – it's awesome. Why separate 'professional' from fun? Some people struggle with that.

As a result, it's now unlikely that, with that attitude, Kimeera is going to get work with the Department of Trade and Industry. But for those that 'get it,' it's clearly a way of separating themselves from every other creative agency.

I caught up with director and *Kimeera Dance Champion* Eddie Johnson and asked him why they did it. "We love having fun in our offices. It makes us damn creative. In some respects it's like a throwback to the old dotcom days. The difference is: we're a real business with real customers. The dancing competition wasn't really ever about dancing or a competition. It was about us showing the world that Kimeera is a fun company, which will think outside the box to make people sit up and take notice."

There's even a sequel, featuring yours truly in a titanic dance-off with Eddie, which had a viral impact across the 4Networking forum, *www.4networking.biz/dance*.

In a bigger way this is how Richard Branson does things. Granted, I'm not too hot at abseiling down buildings and I don't have the budget to 'dick about' in a balloon that can touch the outskirts of space. Does anyone doubt Branson's professionalism or his competence as a business person? Of course not.

So, reframe your thinking.

The business benefits can far

outlive any embarrassment.

Because quirky is unique in your market place.

I've heard on the grapevine that some say I'm "not professional" as a result of my 'free marketing'.

Hang about?

Fastest growing business breakfast network the world has ever seen.

200+ linked groups across the UK and an organisation that's actively making a positive impact to all it touches. That's pretty professional in my book.

I'm not suggesting that everyone should start lugging around hat stands and tennis rackets to networking meetings just to make a point, but why not go for the most extreme hook you can use and feel comfortable with?

Free Jaffa Cakes is an entry level into 'being different' that you could start off with to get people talking. I promise you that once you start on this path, it opens up an entirely new world to you, your business and its marketing.

That's what it's all about. Conversational strategy.

A web designer I now work with calls himself *Spiderman* and wears the superhero's mask at meetings when he does the 40-second stand uppy bit. It's a bit of fun, gets attention and makes a dry subject less dry. The alternative is to talk about PHP, CMS and other ZZZ TLAs.

Do cheap business cards work, does cheap marketing work?

All these things work, if applied correctly, but generally, cheap means crap. I work things out. If a business has a cheap (crap) website and has paid no money or attention to its cards, I come to the conclusion that that's how they operate. That is, crappily and cheaply.

Make a difference with your business card, do something funky. I've got plastic credit card ones which have a totally wacky picture of me winking with a pizza box.

Voice mail: change it now, get people talking. If you've heard mine, it goes something like this:

"Hi, you're through to Brad Burton, the motivational man with the deep pan. I'm probably out delivering pizzas right now, so please leave your order and a message and I'll get back to you."

Guess what? Everyone leaves an 'order' and more often than not the callers are laughing like hell when they leave their message. I've lost count of the number of times someone rings me just so their friend can hear my message.

Once again, what's the downside?

You have to live and breathe your differences. So you have to do something you're comfortable with, something that works.

Beware what your business card, website etc may be saying silently about you and your business practice.

Hand-made business cards are shoddy. Even worse are those manually guillotined cards.

I'm all for being different, but *Sexyguy1973@hotmail. co.uk* is not a great contact detail to have on a card. Whereas, *smile@4networking.biz* is. It's different, funky and effective.

By now, it should be clear that being different isn't all about pizza boxes and pink cowgirl hats with pigtails (although that can help). It's about doing something that generally costs nothing to implement, other than balls out. Someone talking about you, positively or negatively, means it's working.

It's not gone yet, but there is talk of me retiring the pizza box shortly. Everything in life has a shelf-life and I may quit whilst I'm ahead. Like any new chapter, it's just a turn of the page away: perhaps there's another prop gimmick just waiting to happen.

Which brings me nicely onto...

CHAPTER 14
Rubik's Cube

How infuriating are Rubik's Cubes? The world's top-selling puzzle game. You know the one.

You get four sides perfect, but the remaining two stay totally messed up.

Argghh...

As you work on getting the remaining sides with all the colours aligned, you find yourself just a few moves from complete success and yet straight back to all six sides being messed up.

Right now, I'll bet you'd be happy to get back to four completed sides, before attempting again to get it all perfect. In panic mode now, with a flick of the wrist here, a flick of the wrist there, you plough on, rotating the sides. Blind faith and wishful thinking might just sort it, but it's an outside shot.

Great...

You need to

STOP. IMMEDIATELY.

Our story is based on a toy; but try applying this as a metaphor to your business...Your business being a parallel to a Rubik's Cube. You probably want perfection and by wanting that, you run the risk of creating a big old steaming and smelly mess.

Perfection in business is a dangerous goal, but it's also tantalisingly close.

The real secret is to know when perfection is required, and when 'good enough' is, in fact, good enough.

Boeing 737 maintenance engineers require perfection. You probably don't, unless of course you work for Boeing.

I'd like perfection. But it's unrealistic and not actually helpful for you and your business.

Aaryn Warner, founder of online retailer Baer Voce, shares her early experiences in pursuit of perfection in business.

"When I was younger, I hit on a business idea and spent the next 12+ months doing a lot of research and preparation. Target market, pricing, branding...

I wanted everything to be 'perfect' for when I launched the business.

I wouldn't settle for anything less. As time went on, I would have to 'revisit' numerous areas of research because the original research had become outdated. This circular pattern went on for ages. Ultimately, I got what I wanted.

The perfect business

Zero customer care problems – because the business had never had any customers.

Zero financial hiccups – because the business didn't make a bean.

It is a business which remained perfectly untried & perfectly untested: in the only place it could remain perfect...in my imagination.

Then my imagination got bored and life moved on. It makes me wonder just how many businesses have never even been launched because the would-be owner wasn't yet sufficiently mature in their business outlook to set the bar according to what their experience & resources could actually deliver...

Maybe, at that time, I had something in common with people who buy a Rubik's Cube but never play with it because they don't want to mess the colours up: afraid they'll never be able to get it back to being 'perfect' again. Something designed to be an interactive learning game is then treated as a static ornament."

The lesson, "don't get it perfect, just get it going," stands.

I was intrigued by this whole 'perfection paralysis' and the things that go on in our heads as much as in our business. I met with Lisa Blackler of Honesty Marketing, *www.honestymarketing.co.uk*, who I know is big on detail.

Here's Lisa's take on this:

"I am a perfectionist; I get crippled by it. I find myself doing nothing rather than not doing something perfectly. With Honesty Marketing, that could be the temptation with marketing the business – with very little budget I can't do what I believe I should be doing, so I find myself fiddling about trying to find ways to do the right thing. Then I give myself a talking-to and do the things I can do.

One thing is sure: beating yourself up for not achieving perfection is a quick way to misery. Act and something will happen. Standing still is rarely a wise option."

'Perfection paralysis' is a variation of 'dicking about', but with a halo attached. It feels marginally OK because it feels like you are doing something constructive rather than watching TV, but in all likelihood there's as much nutritional content for the brain as in my glory days experiences with Jeremy Kyle.

Whatever road you are on, no matter how much planning you do, there are going to be mess ups. Once you accept that, you are in a much better position to get off your arse and make things happen.

I can vividly recall the pressure during my bad old days of the mortgage payments going out of the bank in 3 days... but without the money in the account to pay for it.

Hairy times indeed. I felt I needed to keep moving: making appointments, seeing potential clients, if only to pacify the wife. It's like this in corporate: we have daft short term targets to hit, which actually do more harm in the medium-to-long term.

What I really needed to do was to *stop moving*. It doesn't mean that I should have stopped completely; as I've always advocated "do something, anything", but the something I needed to do back then was get Zen-like on my own account.

Take stock, chill and get focused.

Having more appointments and making more calls on that basis just meant more opportunities to get things wrong. By foisting myself onto potential clients in that panicked mindset, they sussed out my desperation and people don't buy desperation.

So that was wasted effort.

I also need you to accept that, whatever circumstances you are in that mean you 'need the job', all you can do is give it your best shot.

Which may just require five minutes time out to

STOP – THINK – MOVE

I understand and need you to understand that I understand (got that?) that you may be hungry for a job. In fact you may be starving for a job. I've been there, so that's how I understand and know just what that feels like. You can only give it your best shot. So take five minutes to work out what your best shot is. Stop. Think. Move.

STOP – Tools down. Stop digging. Grab a cup of tea. Take a break.

THINK – Armed with a cup of tea, take stock of where you are. What's the route out of this?

MOVE – OK, five minutes in, with thoughts gathered, proceed. If you find yourself digging a hole, return to **STOP**.

You can't force people to buy from you, but how do you create the conditions to ensure they want to buy from you? Sometimes it's a problem of getting off your arse; sometimes it's a problem of planting the same arse down.

There was one point back in early 2008 where I got us into a Rubik's mess. There were too many hands on the rudder. In fact, that's unfair: we all had different views and consequently, what I failed to do was listen.

As good friend and sales expert Paul McGouran of *www. bespoke-sales-training.co.uk* once told me:

"Two ears, one mouth, one arsehole. Draw your own conclusions."

The key to any business call is to ensure that the team is onboard. That everyone as a collective knows the destination *before* setting off.

A seemingly simple and innocuous decision on my part had disastrous results that reverberated months after the split-second the decision took to make.

It may sound dramatic, but the truth is that we were one passport membership (£490) away from falling over.

A new integrated sales process from Terry and Tamsen, well managed and rapidly rolled out, was the beginning of what was to become our proper training in the membership process. This, combined with steady financial management on the part of Tim Johnson, eventually pulled the 4N nose up from its terminal dive.

You know, now that moment has passed, I wouldn't change a single thing. As a direct result of this, many lessons were learnt, meaning we don't have to endure a similar, maybe critical, 'mistake' in the future.

4N is miles better for it now, but that whole traumatic episode was all based on my refusal not to stop.

Fellas, as in 'menfolk', we've all been there whilst driving around. Stopping and asking for advice is a weakness. We tend to keep ploughing on, even when it's clear to all the passengers that you are driving down the wrong road.

Typical bloke mentality.

"It'll sort itself out if we just keep moving." But generally it doesn't. It just takes you further away from your desired destination. Worse still, you are now low on fuel and in the middle of nowhere.

Had 4Networking fallen over back then, it's unlikely you would be reading this book right now. Conclusion: success and failure are on a parallel path and are very, very close to each other.

However, I do believe you do need to take gambles in business and as a result occasionally make big involuntary mistakes in order to finally succeed.

A mistake is only a mistake after the event. Up until that point it's the correct decision.

No one ever wakes up and thinks, "You know what? I'm going to f*ck up today!"

These cock-ups allow for fresh starts with a different, yet informed perspective.

Gill Bray of Business Hat, *www.businesshat.co.uk*, says:

"In business, it's about calculated risk: the difference between an explorer who takes off with some kit, a bit of intelligence and the determination to get there, and some tit who's gone for a day out to climb Everest with plimsolls, a plastic *pac-*

a-mac and a promise to be back for tea."

Now, I'm not suggesting we all turn into planning and process junkies before we tackle the metaphorical Rubik's Cube...Hang about, once you reach a certain size of business, yes, I am suggesting some planning and process. One quick and incorrect move within a larger organisation can take a disproportionate amount of time to put right. It's a bit like a kid's toy: once it's out of the box, putting it back in is nigh on impossible.

Different departments need to filter the message back through and make things happen. We've all heard that moving larger businesses is akin to turning an oil tanker; I know that all too well. A painful lesson indeed, as a business transitions from being a fleet-of-foot young business and becomes one, up to a point, dependent on processes and planning.

Nobody warned me about that.

In the early exciting days, weeks, months and years, there needs to be an optimum sweet spot between activity and planning on-the-fly. From my experience, as a company matures, the time required for planning will inevitably increase.

By now, you have probably gathered that I look at business as a puzzle and so should you.

Puzzles should be challenging, yet fun, as you look to solve them.

We can't just sit there all day scared of making a call. Oh no, but there is a level of thinking that someone needs to do. Ask my Tim. In the early days, he would talk about me laying fire down-range, machine-gun style. A wonderfully powerful metaphor which creates an image in the mind's eye, the only time I'd stop was to feed in another belt of metaphorical bullets.

80% hit rate in terms of my ability to make decisions, which, when combined with sheer weight of fire, amounts to a lot of positive activity.

Right now, as a result of experience, I reckon my hit rate on calls has increased to around 95%, with even more fire put down-range, as I now have the resource to make things happen.

I've learned something from each of those missed shots. It's not perfection and it doesn't have to be. The problem now, however, is that the 5% that misses can now create absolute chaos for our more established business.

"Oops, I think I just deployed a nuclear warhead and *Hiroshima'd the wrong target.*"

We've now reached a point where the 4N *Diplomat Directors* (the ones whose names begin with 'T'…) earn their wages sorting out my mess. So on the big calls, I now include them in the decision-making process. It's in my interest to get a concurring opinion from the board before pressing the red button in haste.

There's a running joke at 4NHQ, about Tim Johnson metaphorically walking alongside me in a field and picking up a stick.

I say, "You've got the wrong end there, Tim."

He says, "But there's shit on the other end."

I say, "Yeah, I know."

Tim 'Shitty-end-of-the-stick' Johnson. It wasn't that I constantly intended to give him that end of the stick, but that I didn't have the correct attributes or skills to be peacemaker after a mistaken blue-on-blue nuclear attack. It's all about the teams.

Four sides of the Rubik's Cube right. Happy with that? Or do you really want all six?

So, change ONE thing at a time. Sounds a little bit processy for my liking. I've moved from being someone who most definitely had a shoot-first, ask-questions-later mentality, to learning that when your biz reaches a certain size and a certain level, you have to make sure you have the right target before launching a missile.

Test and measure. That may take one day or it may take a week. There is no point in rushing it, especially if potentially it could be a business critical decision.

There will be distractions too. Don't panic. Take stock. You may have a mortgage payment or an invoice that needs paying tomorrow. If you ain't got the money, you ain't got the money. I could have been in the circus, with the amount of invoice-juggling I did in my early days of business.

Balancing suppliers can be an absolute nightmare. Pressure every day, when it comes to tax/VAT man demands: avoid messing with them!

Since this slowdown, they seem to be a lot more amenable and understanding. So if there is a problem on the horizon, speak to them before they speak to you.

"How come I achieved massively in corporate, yet I'm failing as a small business owner?"

The sword and shield that served you so well in corporate are no longer effective. Your world has moved on: the thing that kept you in the clear when the rounds of redundancies kicked in is now actively holding you back. You need to let go of 'that thing'.

Computer – Human

Software – Brain

So why hang on to old programs that don't serve us anymore?

You have to adapt. You wouldn't use Windows 3.1 in business anymore: the same goes for elements of your corporate thinking. Your suit of armour, aka cufflinking, just won't serve you anymore.

The knowledge, skills and experience you picked up when you worked in corporate life are not all obsolete: you just need to take time to look at them and find out what should be wiped from your neuro hard drive and what new versions should be updated and uploaded.

You can't just rely on old software if everyone else in your field is using new versions.

Another solution I worked at recently was with a business owner of a £10 million turnover, 50+ employee outfit, dealing directly with the MD. One of his problems was that productivity was down. He partially attributed this to his employees "wasting company time each day on *Facetube.*"

The great thing about being employed is that if you can't be bothered working, you just pretend, and you still get paid. BRILL!

I got him to accept and recognise that his staff is going to use Facebook, Twitter etc in work time, whether he likes it or not. And if managed correctly, he could actually use their embracing of social media to the advantage of his company.

If you can't beat 'em, join 'em; by rebranding social media 'dicking about' as 'extra marketing resource'. The staff appreciated it and took great pride in promoting the company online when appropriate.

So, accept that just because you pay employees for eight hours a day, they don't work for eight hours. They are humans. Not replicants from *Blade Runner*.

Treat people like idiots, they'll behave like them.

How do you go about resolving the puzzle of "not enough hours in the day"? I've had that asked a couple of times. "Keep a diary and write in it every 15 minutes between one and five words describing what you done."

I promise you that at some point during the average working day, you'll find a few entries of 'dicking about'. There's your solution.

As Steve Lundy, *www.thatchedhotel.co.uk*, hotelier to the stars, shares with us,

"I learned how to do the Rubik's Cube when I was about 18. Even when I knew the secret, I still wanted to do it faster and find better ways to do it, but one thing remained constant and only those who have ever succeeded will understand this...

You get to a point where you have done quite a lot of it, but to get it done completely, you have to mess up a lot of the work you have already done before it all clicks miraculously into place.

Most businesses are no different. You put in the effort, the time, the heartache and the cash. Then you get to a point where one aspect just isn't quite as you wanted it. Having the courage to take that bit and say "Sod it! Let's start that again" and take a step backwards before you go forwards, can be a massive leap of faith but hugely rewarding."

The final puzzle in this chapter and one that I hear most often:

"How do I increase sales?"

I hear it every day and I've already mentioned the solution. It's the *Billy Bear* ham syndrome — draw business to you by delivering value and deploying it, rather than pushing, peddling or shamelessly promoting.

Always try to put yourself in the shoes of the buyer.

Reduce fear. Value is in the eye of the purchaser not the seller.

Make products out of services.

Create desire and stuff sells itself.

You know with Rubik's Cubes, there's a way where you can pull the stickers off and 'solve' the puzzle by cheating. In your business you can also do this, but there comes a point when you've not learned a thing.

Cheating's OK once in a while, but to really progress to the next level, you have to solve the puzzles *in* your business in order to solve the puzzles *of* your business.

Thomas Edison: "I never failed once. It just happened to be a 2000 step process."

Let there be light.

Enjoy those times when you're stumped, when you're not

sure which way to turn, and understand that every mistake moves you on a stage towards your light bulb moment.

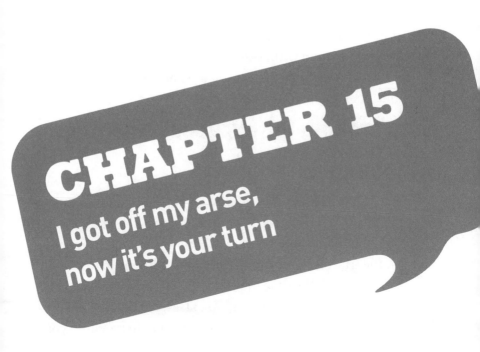

CHAPTER 15

I got off my arse, now it's your turn

There's a real sense of pride when you get off your arse and make something happen, especially when others said, *"It'll never work."*

I should explain, as I begin to write this final chapter, that my life was busy as hell before I even started on this project. There were tens of reasons why tackling this book, my first, was stupid. I nearly talked myself out of it at one point, citing reasons like "no time", other projects and so on.

Now, as I'm on the home straight, how glad do you think I am that I somehow found the time? Chuffed to bits: I'm so excited!

Before the book, I'd been balancing my time, allocating 50% to work, 50% to family. So where was the percentage coming from needed to complete this book within the allocated ten weeks?

I think it helped that work and family/social life are all neatly rolled into one with 4Networking.

Even so, something had to give somewhere, in order to make this book happen.

Stop looking for excuses and things will happen.

One of my friends, Jay, works for an international business and heads up the European arm. He earns well in excess of £150,000 plus bonuses each year. Obscene amounts of money and yet, the truth is, he is deeply unhappy with his lot.

He's on call all the time to ruthless US taskmasters and gets dragged around the world, flying first class, of course. I'm sure it's pretty glamorous those first few times, but after a while you just want your own bed.

Jay has meetings with people around the globe that he has nothing in common with; he doesn't like them or their values and he punts products he doesn't really believe in.

Granted, he has a walk-in wardrobe full of £175 Armani jeans he doesn't wear and a ride-on lawnmower he rarely uses, for the big garden he never sits in. His bank balance earns more interest every month, providing more money than he can sensibly spend.

LIVING THE DREAM.

It's akin to sitting next to an open fire whilst crying: "It burns! It hurts!"

"Well, move away from the fire, Jay, if it's painful."
"But Brad, it provides warmth."

As I see it, Jay has two options:

1. Continue to be an unhappy corporate pawn for the rest of his life, taking his big safety-net salary, until something changes. He'll either get promoted, going further into an organisation he doesn't care about, or get sussed as being deeply unhappy, become mistrusted and ultimately get fired.

2. Start his own business and in doing so take an initial massive dip in income, but be master of his own destiny.

Honestly, when we talk about it, I think Jay is in love with the romantic vision of being self-employed: he comments how, in a nice way, he's envious of me and what I've achieved.

That may be the case now, but five years ago, while he was quaffing champagne & canapés on Virgin Atlantic to New York, I was sipping on own brand teabags and eating Tesco's *Value* fish finger butties while scrabbling down the back of the sofa in the vain hope of finding some loose change.

Jay is not prepared to take the initial drop required to make his own business happen; and you know what? I get it! He's too far in and that's a lot to walk away from.

He's fearful of getting off his arse and changing things, because it'll effectively mean starting over again.

Unfortunately the curse of corporate strikes again, with someone sticking with a job, not for love, but for money.

In golden handcuffs.

If he gave this all up to start a business, he'd no longer have frequent flyer Air Miles building up each month and would have to 'downgrade' from his six bedroom farmhouse to a more modest four bedroom detached. /shudders

He's rather hoping that a 'soft landing fairy' will appear who will give him his first three year contract, which will cover his costs and risks for a business that doesn't exist yet as any more than a wish.

And I want a mortgage that pays itself and a wife that makes cups of tea when I press a button on her forehead. It doesn't work like that.

Neil Jackman, *www.WhitesAndSmalls.co.uk*, says:

"I researched, planned, set a target date and resigned from my job. I sacrificed the good salary and company car for self-employment just over a year ago and it has been tough, but the business is beginning to work.

"Although it's not absolutely essential right now, I am taking the opportunity to dip back into employment on a part-time basis to cover a maternity leave for six months. This means that the salary will cover my monthly living costs and the wages I would have taken from the business can stay in the business to invest in marketing/SEO/further development.

"In principle I like the soft landing option, BUT in reality I'm not sure it works the same — it's like learning to swim in the shallow end. You don't truly learn and gain confidence until you can't touch the bottom of the pool — it adds that extra motivation and determination to reach the edge of the pool!

"I don't think my business would be where it is now if I'd done it part-time/half-heartedly/with a safety net. I think I may have given up and stayed with the easier option."

By the same rule, how great will Jay feel in a few years' time with his own successful business under his belt? Of course, there's a chance he could fail, but then he could go right back into corporate again.

If it all went wrong and he had to re-enter the world of employment, maybe he'd have to slum it in those early days, back on a *mere* £50-80k.

But at least he'd know.

The employee mentality is that the company is responsible for everything and if shit does happen, it is probably the company's fault, but they have a duty to look after me anyway. And if it all goes wrong, the employee can always quit and move on.

Self-employment is where you realise the true nature of life and business.

It's not fair and there is no justice. There is no super-umbrella to protect you from the elements. All you have is yourself, your support team, your wits and determination.

No matter how tough it gets, you don't have the option of quitting. This is what keeps you ploughing on when you hit choppy seas.

The consequences of waiting, for Jay, are continued frustration, increased doubt in his 'real' business ability, and uncertainty.

You know something? I truly admire Jay for what he's achieved. Like me, he's come up from a tough Manchester council estate background, left school early and managed, through a series of calls and decisions, to work his way into a senior corporate position, which is well in excess of what I ever achieved as a 'staffer'. I have *just as much respect* for someone who has left a secure job to follow a dream and who finds themselves struggling to grind out a £15,000 turnover in that first year.

Through my eyes, my topsy-turvy way of looking at the world, I see the self-employed person as an equally successful and yet braver person than the 'unhappy corporate highflyer' pulling the £150,000 salary.

Remember Virgin? You know; the multi-billion pound business with all the trappings associated with success. That didn't start off with someone playing it safe.

For some, uncertainty can be an adrenalin rush, for others it's poison.

The fact that you are reading this book means that deep down, coasting is not an option.

Action is what generates success and progress.

Doing stuff, even imperfect stuff, moves you on.

Once the final pages of this book are turned, it's over to you, to draw upon your own resources.

Self leadership

This is taken directly from the *4Networking Manual*, written by Network Director Tamsen Garrie:

"Self-leadership: it's the capacity and the commitment to take responsibility and create outcomes that are meaningful to *you*. It is the opposite of shifting responsibility for those outcomes onto other people or circumstances.

Learning to lead ourselves is a challenge.

But it is an essential capability, as it is what enables us to not only achieve our own goals, but also to understand how we can inspire others to do it for themselves.

We are not motivated by others.

Motivation is an inside job; and what leaders do is to help others to identify and tap into what is important to them, so that they are personally motivated to go the extra mile.

Ultimately, it always starts with you."

Going forward, from this day onwards, don't talk yourself out of anything.
Talk yourself into things.

The Space Shuttle needs massive boosters full of fuel (energy) in order to launch it into orbit. Equally, you will also: no point in boosting for a bit and then taking your foot off the gas. You need to commit to keeping your boosters on and you must not switch them off until you are in successful business orbit.

Create positive and lasting momentum. In your mind, you are going to need it for the journey ahead. Find yourself having more 'make it happen Mondays' rather than 'can't be bothered Tuesdays'.

Draw on the support of those around you: collaborative working.

Share resources. Never stand still.

Throughout the journey you are soon to embark on, there'll be times when you'll wonder if you would have been better suited to Billy Smart's circus: juggling finances, spinning plates, which at times are as wobbly as hell, but as long as they don't actually fall over, wobbly is OK.

Enjoy the excitement, savour the risk.

Because, when you break through, that excitement and risk will be replaced with stability and a solid business model that people admire.

In business, if you are not shouting about yourself, no one else will be.

Get loud, win attention, win new friends and win new business.

Win.

Get involved with 4Networking and see it for what it is: it's not just another network.

It's really not: it's a Get Off Your Arse *movement*. It's a place of fun, a place of work, a place to belong; and it's an organisation that lives and breathes the lessons and teachings of this book.

Right at the heart of it is a unique culture, awash with energy, vibrancy and ideas, all bound together with a working ethos of support for each other. It's like a big ship, with the gearing locked on full speed ahead.

Every member is an active passenger on the vessel, moving forward with us.

With 4N, you create a transferable network which transcends the boundaries of the conventional networking thinking of 'winning business.'

Boring... I want a network that's life-changing!

As a collective, all of a sudden, all our small businesses

have a voice, a big one.

It's the real Business Link between employment and self-employment.

I'll go on record and say that this book, like 4Networking before it, will shake up the business/networking scene forever. You are part of that shake up: as a thought leader, a pioneer of this honest approach to business, networking and people. Please tell someone about this book and its message across the UK and beyond: *Get Off Your Arse!*

Let's make a difference not only to ourselves, but to all those we meet.

Let's get the UK moving.

4Networking supports: it provides guidance and answers and is a brilliant social and business platform for people like you, me and Jay whilst ideas and companies are formed. Our unique culture and genuine understanding of the challenges that small businesses face each and every day will give you a massive advantage. After all, I've been there, we all have!

Ultimately, it's still down to you to utilise it. Without responsibility, ownership, commitment and motivation (self-leadership), it is just a platform, a culture, some tools available to you.

On the field of battle, I'd rather go out through a head shot, not a leg wound, knowing I had given it my best.

In life, we stay with things because it's easy: relationships that are going nowhere; networks that are outdated and don't work; jobs and people that we don't love or even like; all for the easy life.

But rarely is this route really the easy life. It's the hard one, long-term.

Starting your own business isn't easy.

Changing the direction of your life is scary.

But in this book I've shared with you the highs and the lows of doing both.

But for you to see life truly in Technicolor, a world where you can be creative, a world where you can actually start being you, the real you, not somebody squashed into a space created by someone else, with somebody else's values, then you have to walk the path of hard, the life of scary, at least at the beginning.

But what I can tell you is as hard and as scary as my journey was back then:

I wouldn't change a single thing: it's made me what I am.

Start your own business, stick with it through those tough times and take control of your life once and for all.

Have the attitude that you would rather live in a caravan than go back to working as an unhappy corporate slave living a grey life.

You are in the right job when you look forward to 'working', because it's no longer a chore, it's something you enjoy.

We are in the right relationship when we reveal our true selves to those around us and we are still loved.

Get these two right and it really is the easy life, as you are inspired to do more.

Take control of your destiny today and change the things that are making you unhappy or are holding you back.

Make that call and live with the outcome.

If you don't do it today, you'll probably never do it.

The consequence of waiting for the perfect moment is that you find it will never happen. I can't do your press-ups for you, it's up to you.

Embrace your dream or abandon it and do something else.

My daft idea and my dream was: to make a difference.

Hopefully, by reading this book, you'll see I'm living proof that daft ideas, like dreams before them, can come true.

There really aren't any shortcuts to success.

Don't reach the end of your life to find yourself sitting in a chair overlooking the sea thinking, "If only".

You have one life. Don't fritter it away and have an unhappy, compromised life.

Have no regrets.

Go for it.

Please contact me if this book has in some way helped you move forward.

If you manage to bump into me, let's have a 10 minute appointment: after all, you just don't know where it may lead.

Brad@getoffyourarse.biz

So turn this page and...

Kick your brain into action and start enjoying wins where you can. Join me on our journey, to make a massive and positive difference to your life and that of those you love. Simply...

Acknowledgements

People who helped me Get Off My Arse will probably help you get off yours too! (aka free plugs):

Look how **4Networking members** have helped to make this book happen; effectively creating one of those virtual companies which I talked about earlier.

Tim Johnson – Director of Strategy – 4Networking. Sharp operator, a highly tuned brain; perfect if you want help. *www.scaleyourbiz.co.uk* : look him up.

Terry Cooper – Development Director – 4Networking. He's got 30 years' worth of ties for sale, as he no longer needs them. He's also got 30 years of PLC & sales experience: *www.cooperbradbury.co.uk*

Tamsen Garrie – Network Director – 4Networking. My first foray into removing self-limiting beliefs started with a session with Tam. If you've got a business, a brain and a block you probably need *www.alpha-associates.biz*

Cover design & page setting by **Paul Williams** from **Extrabold Design**: *www.extrabolddesign.com*

Helped along with a brainwave cover concept nod all the way from Australia-based friend & movie poster designer **Jeremy Saunders**: *www.jeremysaunders.com*

Gill Bray from **Business Hat** *www.businesshat.co.uk* undertook the labour of love first edit for me and kept me gee'd up by assuring me I was right on track with her love of the whole book.

Karen Longstaff & **Paul Norman** from **Orange Tree Development** *www.orangetreedevelopment.co.uk* developed the *www.getoffyourarse.biz* website.

Mindy Gibbins-Klein *www.bookmidwife.com* helped me to pull this book concept out of my head and supported me with a three month programme which ensured I stayed on time, schedule and on message. She can do the same for you!

Mark Beaumont-Thomas *www.lexiconmarketing.co.uk*, for final editing, grammar etc, whilst retaining the Manc intact. If you are serious about your online presence, check out his other company: *www.profilebuilder.co.uk*

Stef Thomas *www.noredbraces.co.uk*: The marketing genius behind the erm, marketing strategy for GOYA.

Mira Taylor – finally a Public Relations company that over-delivers every time…*www.avidpr.co.uk* handles 4Networking, my personal and GOYA PR.

Nick Hill *www.binaryvision-nlp.com*: The Wizard of NLP improved my stage presence, breathing, presentation skills and does his magic to ensure that nerves are replaced with great confidence when on stage.

GET OFF YOUR ARSE

Justin Dodd *www.evolvetraininguk.co.uk*: Personal trainer who helps with my bacon retention & is a bodyguard providing close protection from my hordes of female groupies...

Priscilla Morris *www.loudandclearuk.com*: Vocal coach who helped me sound less Noel Gallagher and more Peter Kay, trust me that's a good thing!

Mikey Palmer *www.michaelpalmer.com*: My official photographer. Coo.

Robin Parker *www.ccprinting.co.uk*: Printing this awesome book, at a typically awesome price.

Jeff Peyton-Bruhl and **Martin Wilson** at **Hyundai Motor UK Ltd Corporate Operations** *www.hyundai.co.uk* for their belief in 4Networking and their great cars.

Rebecca Burn-Callander, for being a hot Billie Piper lookalike and for being you. Read my column in *www.realbusiness.co.uk*.

Look out for me speaking at events hosted by the following organisations, all of which are headed up by top top blokes: *www.businessnorthwest.co.uk, www.business-yorkshire.co.uk, www.business-midlands.co.uk.*

Three Seriously Spectacular business shows in the UK and a really cool pal & MD, **Scott Hider – Nationwide Media Group** *www.nwe.co.uk.*

Mark Linton – The Business Growth Show *www.thebusinessgrowthshow.co.uk.* A network of rolling and FREE one day business/networking shows around the UK.

Warren Cass – Business Scene *www.business-scene.com* A web-based networking portal, which features networking events from up and down the UK.

4Ners who gave GOYA a test drive and full reads: **Julian Wellings** *www.expertiseontap.co.uk*, **Chris Slay** *www.acornrecruitmentsw.co.uk*, **Nick Hutt** *www.justwills-southwest.co.uk*, **Tom Lawrence** *www.tlcbusiness-supplies.co.uk*, **Emily Cagle** *www.emilycagle.co.uk.*

Plus a cast of hundreds of you guys giving me support and guidance; and of course thanks for all the great quotes from 4Networking members up and down the country which are included within the book. I hope I've not missed anyone, but if I have, sorry: remember a mistake is only a mistake after the event!

Anyways, thank you all so much for your belief in me. You can follow my inane ranting on *www.twitter.com/BradBurton*. X

Need a decent GOYA-esque speaker for your event? Do check out *www.speakerseeker.net*: Real Speakers for the Real World.

To book Brad to speak at your event, kick some arse in your business or to enrol yourself on a 1-1 GOYA programme: *www.bradburton.biz* **0845 123 4444**